Mission 17: The Dawn of a New Day

Someon… showed us… courage a… strength… took to overcome adversity in life.

ENTER

DO NOT ENTER

SAY WHAT? THE ROAD'S OUT?

......

The four of us were old friends. We'd planned this getaway as a graduation present to ourselves.

Actually, we were just trying to run away from our problems.

I knew it wouldn't do any good. We all did, actually.

Then, it happened.

It was so sudden--straight out of the blue.

WAUGH!

WHUMP

SCREECH
......
I HIT HIM.

THEN, *WE'LL* TAKE HIM.
WE CAN'T MOVE HIM. SUPPOSE HIS BACK'S BROKEN.
I'M FINE.

I'M ALL RIGHT.
HURRY UP AND GO.
ALL... ALL RIGHT?
BUT... BUT... HOW?
YOU'RE *HURT.*
IT'S NOTHING.
THE ROAD'S OUT UP AHEAD.
GO BACK THE WAY YOU CAME.

Someone showed us the courage and strength it took to overcome adversity in life.
I doubt anybody will ever believe our story.
We even have a hard time believing it-- and we were there.
The person came out of nowhere.
Yet, that person changed our outlook on life-- *forever*-- in just one night.

Mission 17: THE DAWN OF A NEW DAY

WHAT AN AWESOME SUNSET.
WHAT DO YOU KNOW? IT STOPPED RAINING.
I'D PROBABLY EVEN FEEL GOOD--IF IT WEREN'T FOR *THAT*.
SNAP

Besides, everyone's in the cottage.
WHO AM I KIDDING? ONLY IDIOTS LIKE US WOULD COME TO THE MIDDLE OF NOWHERE ON OUR VACATION.
MAN, I SURE AM HUNGRY.
That's odd. I'd swear there was someone there.
HEY--IS SOMEONE THERE?
SUZU-KO?
Koto-ne...
Koto-ne...

Koto-ne...
I've always thought you were special.
Will you go out with me?
Hey, look! We both passed.
We can go to the same senior high school together, too.
1031
1033
1039
1042
1043
1047
1051 22 143
1052 1126 143
I'm... sorry.
Really.
I'm sorry, Koto-ne.
She's... um...
ZONING OUT AGAIN, KOTONE?
THINKING ABOUT TORU--AGAIN?
FORGET ABOUT THAT TWO-TIMING LOSER!

MY PARENTS ARE GOING TO SPLIT-- AND THEY'VE BEEN MARRIED FOR 30 YEARS. YOU SHOULD SEE THE MESS THERE.
YOU WENT OUT WITH HIM FOR A LONG TIME SO IT'S HARD TO FORGET. I CAN RELATE.
BUT, NEVER, EVER TRUST ANYONE-- ESPECIALLY A GUY.
YOU'VE LEARNED A LESSON, NOW MOVE ON.
SURE. IT'S WRITTEN ALL OVER YOUR FACE.
I WASN'T THINKING. NOT ABOUT TORU, ANYWAY.
ARGH! THE GRILL DOESN'T WORK!
Oh, Rin.
THEY'RE FINAL-IZING IT NOW.
LOOKS LIKE IT.
ARE YOUR PARENTS REALLY GOING TO SPLIT?
I knew them when they were still happy together. You must be taking it really hard.
THOSE TWO GUYS CAN'T, THOUGH.
But, Rin...
I'M NOT A KID ANYMORE. I CAN HANDLE IT.
WHOOMPH
Finally. It's on!
BUT, HEY, THEY CAN DO WHAT-EVER THEY WANT.

We all have our own problems that we can't do anything about.

I guess other people might consider them trivial. But, for us, they're anything but.

They're painful. So, we're running away from them. We just want to forget--if only for just a little while.

I STILL CAN'T BELIEVE NOTHING'S GONE OUR WAY.
But, there's still no light at the end of the tunnel.
WHY DID WE HAVE TO BRING THAT PIECE OF "BAGGAGE" HERE?!
SOME PEOPLE GET NOTHING BUT BAD BREAKS!
THAT WAS UNCALLED FOR. WE DECIDED--
RIN!
LOOK! I'M REALLY ANGRY WITH JUN, TOO!
WHY'D THAT HALF-WIT RENT THIS RUNDOWN COTTAGE, WHICH IS IN THE MIDDLE OF NOWHERE I MIGHT ADD?!
I SHOULDN'T HAVE LET HIM MAKE THE ARRANGEMENTS.
GIMME A BREAK, SUZUKO! THIS WAS THE ONLY THING WE COULD AFFORD!
TAKASHI'S WITH HIM. MAYBE HE'S PATCHIN' HIM UP NOW.
CHOMP
WAIT A SECOND!
THEN, WHO'S WITH HIM?! YOU DIDN'T LEAVE HIM BY HIMSELF, DID YOU?!
I'M HUNGRY. WHEN'S DINNER?
Omelets? ♡ Right on!
I THOUGHT YOU WERE UPSTAIRS.
I WAS CHECKING AROUND OUTSIDE, SINCE IT STOPPED RAINING.

CAN HE DEAL WITH IT BY HIMSELF? IT'S OUR FAULT IF HE TAKES A TURN FOR THE WORSE, YOU KNOW!
NAH, IT SHOULD BE OKAY. HE COMES FROM A FAMILY OF DOCTORS.
NEITHER OF YOU MADE IT INTO MED SCHOOL!
HEY! I SAID DON'T MENTION MED SCHOOL AROUND US!
STOP IT, YOU TWO!
THERE ARE MORE IMPOR-TANT THINGS RIGHT NOW.
HOW ABOUT GIVING SOME THOUGHT TO THE GUY WE BROUGHT HERE?
WE FORCED HIM TO COME HERE. HE DIDN'T WANT TO. REMEMBER?
What?
I'm fine. I can walk from here.
It's not fine. You're bleeding.
Look, we rented a cottage around here. If nothing else, let's get you bandaged up.
I'm fine. Hey!

WE JUST COULDN'T HAVE LEFT HIM THERE.
I SUP-POSE.
BUT, WE COULD'VE TAKEN HIM TO A HOSPITAL!
KOTO-NE?
WE ARE SO SELF-CEN-TERED.
WE WOULD'VE FELT GUILTY IF WE LEFT HIM THERE. BUT, TRUTH BE TOLD...
WE ALL WANTED TO.
WE REALLY DIDN'T BRING HIM HERE TO SEE IF HE WAS ALL RIGHT.
WE DID IT FOR OUR-SELVES--NOT FOR HIM.
I'M JUST TIRED OF ALL THIS. I'M SICK OF IT. WHY ARE WE SO PATHETIC?
WE'RE SO ENGROSSED IN OUR OWN PROBLEMS WE CAN'T EVEN CARE ABOUT SOMEONE WHO'S ACTUALLY HURT.
SLAM

THUD THUD THUD

THUD THU

SLAM

WC

URRRRP

TAKA-SHI?

WHAT'S WITH HIM?

THE CUTS HE HAD...

HE STITCHED THEM UP-- *HIMSELF.*

I TELL YOU.
SOME-THING AIN'T RIGHT ABOUT HIM.
THE GUY WAS WALKING, SO I THOUGHT HE HAD NOTHING BUT MINOR CUTS.
BUT, I TOOK A CLOSER LOOK AND THE GUY'S GOT *SERIOUS* INJURIES.
I WAS THINKING WE'D HAVE TO TAKE HIM TO THE HOSPITAL.
THEN THE GUY PULLS OUT A FIRST-AID KIT.
HE STITCHED UP EVERYTHING.
MAYBE HIS PARENTS ARE DOC-TORS.
Like Takashi's
YOU'RE AN IDIOT.
AND, SUPPOSE THEY WERE. HE'D STILL BE TOO YOUNG TO KNOW WHAT TO DO.
HE LOOKS GIRLY, BUT HE'S ANYTHING BUT.
JUST TAKE A LOOK.
IT'LL BLOW YOUR MIND.

We stopped in our tracks.
For a second, no one could say anything.
The wind blowing through the trees.
The evening air.

It's like our "guest" was a part of the forest.

I don't know what made me think that.

Right away, I could tell our newcomer didn't lead a normal life.

In any case, all of us were left speechless. The person seemed that heavy.

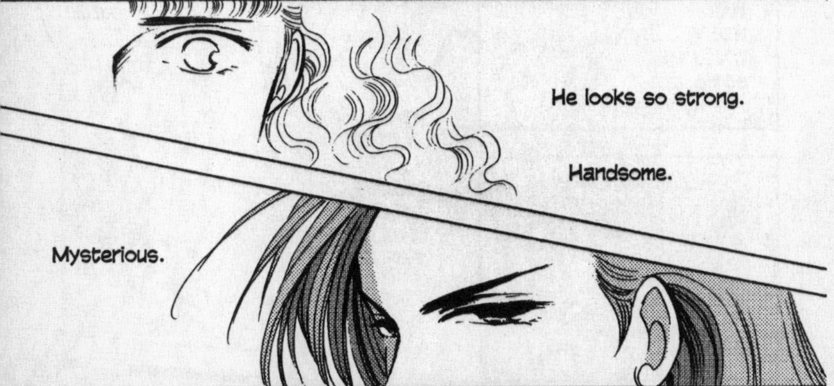
He looks so strong.
Handsome.
Mysterious.

UM...THAT IS THE GUY WE PICKED UP, RIGHT?
HE WAS FILTHY, BUT YEAH. LOOKS TOTALLY DIFFERENT, THOUGH.
UH... YEAH.
HEAD-TURNING. DEFI-NITELY.
YEAH... UM...
I THOUGHT I'D INTRODUCE EVERY-ONE.
I'M TAKASHI. THIS IS JUN.
SHE'S KOTONE. AND, THAT'S SUZUKO.
WE'RE OLD FRIENDS WHO DECIDED TO GET OUT OF TOWN FOR A FEW DAYS.
I'M KOTO-NE.
IF IT MEANS ANYTHING, I'M REALLY SORRY. YOU CAME OUT OF NOWHERE.
YOU SHOULD WATCH WHERE YOU'RE GOING.
RIN!
UM... LOOK.

ARE YOU... UH... OKAY?

YOU DID SOME-THING STUPID.

HUH?

FIRST: YOU DIDN'T LEAVE WHEN YOU HAD THE CHANCE.

SECOND: YOU BROUGHT ME HERE.

"STUPID?!" WE COULDN'T HAVE LEFT YOU THERE!

IT'S TOO LATE NOW.

TOO LATE?

YOU SHOULD HAVE LEFT ME.

NOW, THEY WANT YOU DEAD, TOO.

I SHOULD'VE BEEN MORE INSISTENT BACK THEN.
MAYBE HE HIT HIS HEAD.
OR, HE'S JUST NUTS.
GRAB

WHAT WAS--?!
GET DOWN!
DUCK
RIP
BSH
BSH
BSH
BARRICADE THE WINDOWS! IN THE OTHER ROOMS, TOO!
LOCK THE DOORS! HURRY!
WAUUUGH!

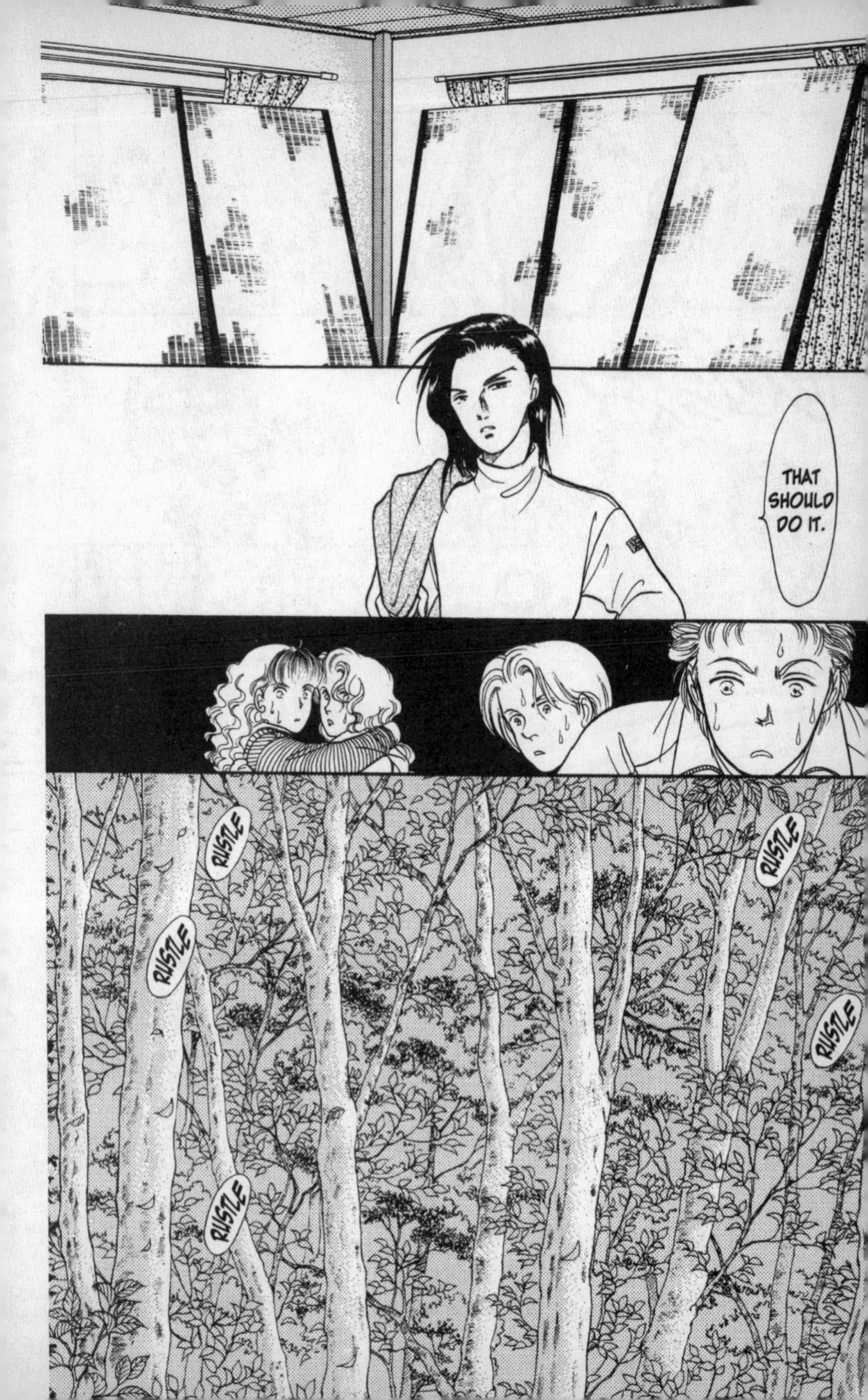
THAT SHOULD DO IT.
RUSTLE
RUSTLE
RUSTLE
RUSTLE
RUSTLE

SO, LET'S GET THIS STRAIGHT.
THE C.I.A. PRETTY MUCH WIPED OUT AN INTERNATIONAL TERRORIST GROUP.
ITS LEADERS WERE HIDING OUT HERE UNTIL THEY COULD MAKE THEIR WAY TO RUSSIA.
YOU CAME HERE TO CATCH THEM.
BUT, WE SHOWED UP IN THE MIDDLE OF A GUN BATTLE.
MORE OR LESS.
I DID TRY TO STOP YOU FROM GETTING CAUGHT IN THE CROSS-FIRE.
IT WAS THE ONLY WAY, SINCE I WASN'T EXPECTING ANYONE UP HERE.
......
THE ROAD WAS BLOCKED OFF, SO WHY DIDN'T YOU TURN AROUND?
......
DOES THAT MAKE YOU A C.I.A. AGENT?
Sort of?

NO. I WORK FOR A DIFFERENT ORGANIZATION. IT DOESN'T BELONG TO ANY SINGLE COUNTRY.
WE TRY TO PRESERVE ORDER IN THE WORLD.
WE GO INTO ACTION WHEN OTHERS NO LONGER CAN.

ANY-THING ELSE?
NAH. YOU TOLD US MORE THAN ENOUGH.
I TOTALLY UNDERSTAND NOW.
BUT, IT IS HARD TO BELIEVE.
IT'S LIKE A BAD, BAD DREAM.
IT'S VERY REAL.
YOU SAW THE BULLET HOLES.

LET'S SAY THIS REALLY IS HAPPENING. HOW MANY OF THEM ARE THERE?
THEY'RE THE LAST FEW SURVIVORS. ABOUT 20 TO 30.
THIRTY?!
HOW MANY OF YOU GUYS ARE THERE?!
DO THEY EVEN KNOW YOU'RE HERE?!
JUST ME. AND, NO.
WHAT?!
I DIDN'T ASK FOR BACKUP.
I CAN DEAL WITH THAT LOT WITHOUT ANY HELP.

HOW? CELL PHONES WON'T WORK HERE! WE'RE NOWHERE NEAR CIVILIZATION!
I HAVE A SATELLITE PHONE IN MY BACKPACK. I'M NEVER OUT OF TOUCH.
A WARNING, THOUGH.
STILL, I DIDN'T COUNT ON RUNNING INTO YOU.
SO, FOR YOUR SAKE, I AM GOING TO CALL FOR BACKUP.
THE FASTEST MY PEOPLE CAN GET HERE IS DAWN.
UNTIL THEN, WE HAVE TO DEFEND OURSELVES.
RUSTLE
RUSTLE
RUSTLE

ARGH!
OF ALL THE PEOPLE WE COULD'VE PICKED UP!
WHY DOES EVERY-THING HAVE TO HAPPEN TO ME?!
NO SENSE IN COM-PLAINING ABOUT IT NOW.
WHAT? YOU TWO ACTUALLY BELIEVE WHAT THAT LOON WAS SELLING?
TERRORISTS?! C.I.A.?! I DON'T THINK SO!
THEN, WHAT ABOUT THOSE BULLET HOLES?
SOME-BODY WAS SHOOTING-- FOR REAL-- AT US.
IF NOTHING ELSE, WE'RE IN BIG TROUBLE. THAT MUCH IS FOR SURE.
TAKA-SHI?
FINISHED CLEANING UP ALREADY? SORRY, WE SHOULD'VE HELPED.
IT'S NOT THAT.
COULD I BORROW A SHIRT? HE NEEDS TO CHANGE.
WHAT ARE YOU TALKING ABOUT? THAT GUY'S BROUGHT US NOTHING BUT BAD LUCK!
STILL...

BLOOD STARTED SEEPING THROUGH WHEN HE WAS TALKING.
I THINK IT'S BECAUSE HE WAS MOVING AROUND AFTER HE WAS SHOT.
Is this one okay?
DIDN'T ANY OF YOU NOTICE?
HE PUT HIS LIFE ON THE LINE TO PROTECT US.
THAT'S ... UM ...
THAT'S *HIS* PROBLEM!
YEAH. IT'S NOT OUR FAULT.
IF ANYTHING, *HE'S* TO BLAME.
I DON'T KNOW WHAT'S GOING ON, BUT THANKS TO HIM LOOK AT THE MESS WE'RE IN.
WE COULD ALL END UP DEAD, YOU KNOW!
FORGET ABOUT HIM. WE HAVE TO FIGURE OUT HOW TO ESCAPE.
WE'RE ALWAYS RUNNING AWAY, AREN'T WE?
HUH?
HE TRIED TO STOP US. REMEMBER? IF WE HADN'T GONE AROUND THE ROADBLOCK, WE WOULDN'T HAVE HIT HIM.
I'M SCARED TO DEATH OF ALL THIS, TOO.
BUT, THAT DOESN'T GIVE ME THE RIGHT TO BE A TOTAL COWARD.

He was anything but.
A regular guy, that is.
The C.I.A.? Terrorists? But, him, I can believe.
Something is...different about him. But, what? He's very mysterious. I'll say that much.
No matter how incredible he may be, he's still a person.
Isn't he scared?
It is strange, though.
Why am I taking this so calmly?
What does he go through every day?
He's young, too.
Is it because it's so unreal it just hasn't struck home yet?
No. That's not it, because I am scared.
Still...

I feel so much safer--
with him around.
Why is that?
Is it because he gives off this sense of invincibility?
What does it take to be so confident?
What does it take to not run away?
What does it take to face up to reality?
What does it take?
I BROUGHT YOU A CHANGE OF CLOTHES.
THANKS.

YOU'RE CHANGING THE DRESSING?
IT HASN'T STOPPED BLEEDING.
NO. I'M USED TO THIS.
CAN I HELP?
HERE, GIVE ME THAT!
......
THANKS.
ARE YOU...
ARE YOU SCARED?
......

I MEAN, PEOPLE ARE TRYING TO KILL YOU.
AND, YOU'RE REALLY HURT.
I'VE BEEN TRAINED TO BLOCK OUT FEAR...AND PAIN.
YOU CAN'T PROTECT THE WORLD IF YOU'RE SCARED.
CAN I ASK YOU SOMETHING *PERSONAL?*
IS THERE...
UM... SOMEONE YOU LIKE?
...
YES.
AS IN LOVE?
YES.
ARE YOU STILL TOGETHER?
NO.

I HAD TO MOVE ON.
OH.
SO WHERE ...?
IN YOUR WORLD.
HOW DO I PUT THIS...
MY OTHER HALF BELONGS IN YOUR WORLD, A WORLD OF RELATIVE PEACE.
THERE'S NO WAY WE COULD'VE STAYED TOGETHER.
BUT...
YOU MUST'VE BEEN IN LOVE.
YES. IT WAS MY FIRST TIME-- AND PROBABLY MY LAST TIME.
WE'LL NEVER SEE EACH OTHER AGAIN. IT HAS TO BE THAT WAY.

I DON'T WANT MY FRIEND TO GO THROUGH WHAT YOU'RE GOING THROUGH.
......
DOESN'T IT HURT?
YOU'RE IN LOVE, BUT YOU CAN'T SEE EACH OTHER? HOW DO YOU DEAL WITH IT?
BY CHANGING HOW I LOOK AT IT.
I NOW VIEW MY MISSIONS AS HAVING DIRECT RELEVANCE TO MY LIFE.
I GUARD THE WORLD MY FRIEND LIVES IN. SO BY EXTENSION, THEY'RE PROTECTED.

I knew it.
He really is strong inside.
I ALMOST FORGOT.
BLOOD'S SEEPING THROUGH. PUT THIS ON AFTER YOU CHANGE THE BANDAGES.
I WILL. THANK YOU.
He's so strong inside.
ONE MORE THING.
IS THAT SOME-ONE SPECIAL JAPANESE?
YES.
ABOUT AS OLD AS YOU.
HE IS VERY SWEET.
WHAT'S TAKING HER SO LONG?
WHAT'S SHE DOIN' UP THERE?
GETTING JEALOUS, ARE WE? YOU WERE SO STOKED SHE WAS SINGLE AGAIN.
BET YOU DIDN'T EXPECT MR. PERFECT TO WALK IN.
SHUT UP!
WE COULD GET KILLED ANYTIME NOW, BUT THAT'S WHAT YOU TWO--
THUD THUD THUD THUD
I CAN'T BELIEVE HOW FLIPPANT YOU IDIOTS ARE.

OH, MAN!
WHAT?
DID HE TRY TO DO SOME-THING TO YOU?
AT A TIME LIKE THIS? WHAT A CREEP!
NO! IT'S NOT THAT!
YOU KNOW THAT GUY?
HE'S A GIRL!
NO WAY!
CREAK
DON'T MAKE ANY NOISE.
TURN OFF THE LIGHTS.

THEY'RE HERE.
I CAN'T TAKE THIS ANY-MORE!

I CAN'T! I JUST CAN'T!
KEEP IT DOWN!
WHY DOES EVERYTHING HAVE TO HAPPEN TO ME? WHY DO I DESERVE THIS?
CALM DOWN!
WHERE'D SHE GO?
UP-STAIRS.
SHE SAID SHE NEEDED TO GET SOME THINGS.
Sure
SHE'S GONNA DITCH US AND MAKE A RUN FOR IT.
HOW CAN YOU SAY THAT?
SHE'S NOT THAT SORT OF PERSON!
THEN, WHAT SORT OF PERSON IS SHE?
WHAT DO YOU REALLY KNOW ABOUT HER?
UM... ER...
IT'S ALL HER FAULT.

SLAP
IT'S ALL BECAUSE OF HER!
IF WE'D JUST LEFT HER, WE'D--!
YOU HEARD ME! EVERYTHING'S HER FAULT!
IF IT WASN'T FOR HER, EVERYTHING WOULD'VE BEEN FINE. EVERYTHING WOULD'VE GONE BACK TO NORMAL!
THERE YOU GO BLAMING SOMEONE ELSE AGAIN!
ARE YOU GOING TO KEEP RUNNING AWAY FOR THE REST OF YOUR LIFE?
IT'S NOBODY'S FAULT BUT OURS!
BECAUSE WE'RE WEAK, WE TRIED TO RUN AWAY FROM OUR PROBLEMS. WE BROUGHT IT UPON OURSELVES.
WE DESERVE IT.
ALL OF YOU KNOW THAT.
I'M NOT GOING TO RUN AWAY ANYMORE.
CREAK
I'M SCARED, BUT I DON'T WANT TO RUN AWAY.
I MIGHT DIE, BUT I'M GOING TO MAKE A STAND.
DON'T WORRY.

I'M HERE.
I'LL DEAL WITH THEM.

DEAL WITH THEM?
......
I'LL BE FINE.
NO!
YOU CAN'T!
YOU'LL GET KILLED!
YOU CAN'T GO!
YOU'RE HURT!
DON'T GO OUT THERE!
YOU'RE OUTNUMBERED!
HELP ME STOP HER!

HELP ME STOP HER BEFORE SHE GETS *KILLED!*
SHE'S GONNA GET KILLED BECAUSE OF *US!*
PLEASE!
STOP RUN-NING AWAY!
DON'T ...
DON'T GO.
STAY HERE.
YEAH. DON'T PUSH IT.
YOU'RE HURT.
HELP'S ON THE WAY, RIGHT?
TAKASHI?
THANK YOU FOR YOUR CONCERN.

HOW DID YOU GET TO BE SO TOUGH?
HOW CAN YOU BE SO BRAVE?
YOU'RE A GIRL-- JUST LIKE ME.
......
HOW ...?
LIKE I SAID, MY MISSIONS ARE IMPORTANT TO ME.
I'LL BE ALL RIGHT. SO, DON'T WORRY.
BUT, IT'LL BE MORE DANGEROUS FOR YOU IF I STAY HERE.
PLEASE TELL ME.
WHAT'S THE SECRET?
NO ONE CAN SHOULDER YOUR PAIN.
BUT, NO ONE CAN STOP YOU FROM LOOKING TO TOMORROW, EITHER.
NO MATTER HOW HARD OR PAINFUL IT IS, HOLD YOUR HEAD UP HIGH.
LOOK TO TOMORROW. NOT OVER YOUR SHOULDER AT YESTERDAY.
......
HOLD YOUR HEAD UP.

ALL OF YOU HAVE A FUTURE.
I'LL SEE TO THAT--PERSON-ALLY.
SLAM
With that, she walked out the door.
The gunfire started right away.
The sound of the gunfire was unbearable. It was right there.
But, I wasn't scared.
I don't think anybody else was either.
I knew why, too.

So do we.
All of us have our own personal demons. In the end, we have to face them alone.
She may have been fighting-- all by herself.
But, she was fighting for us-- and for the person she loved.
She had a reason to fight.
For tomorrow. For us.
CREAK
It's up to us to find the light at the end of the tunnel.
GOOD MORNING.
IT'S ALL CLEAR.

Wow. It's bright out.
THE GIRL...
THE GIRL WHO WAS WITH US. WHERE IS SHE?
ALREADY ON HER NEXT MISSION.
SHE DID LEAVE A MESSAGE, THOUGH.
"THERE WILL ALWAYS BE A TOMOR-ROW."

We all did.

We were fine during the fighting.

I started crying again.

I CAN'T BELIEVE HOW STUPID I-- WE--WERE.

THERE ARE MORE IMPORTANT THINGS OUT THERE.

WE WERE HUNG UP ON SOMETHING COMPLETELY TRIVIAL.

"There will always be a tomorrow.

It's up to you now."

WE'LL COME OUT OF THIS STRONGER.

WE'VE CHANGED.

I JUST KNOW WE WILL.

Toru phoned that day. I told him where he could go.
BUT, YOU'D PROBABLY ALREADY FORGOT-TEN ABOUT HIM.
WAY TO GO!
HAHAHA HAHAHA
YEAH.

I'm not the same person I was yesterday.

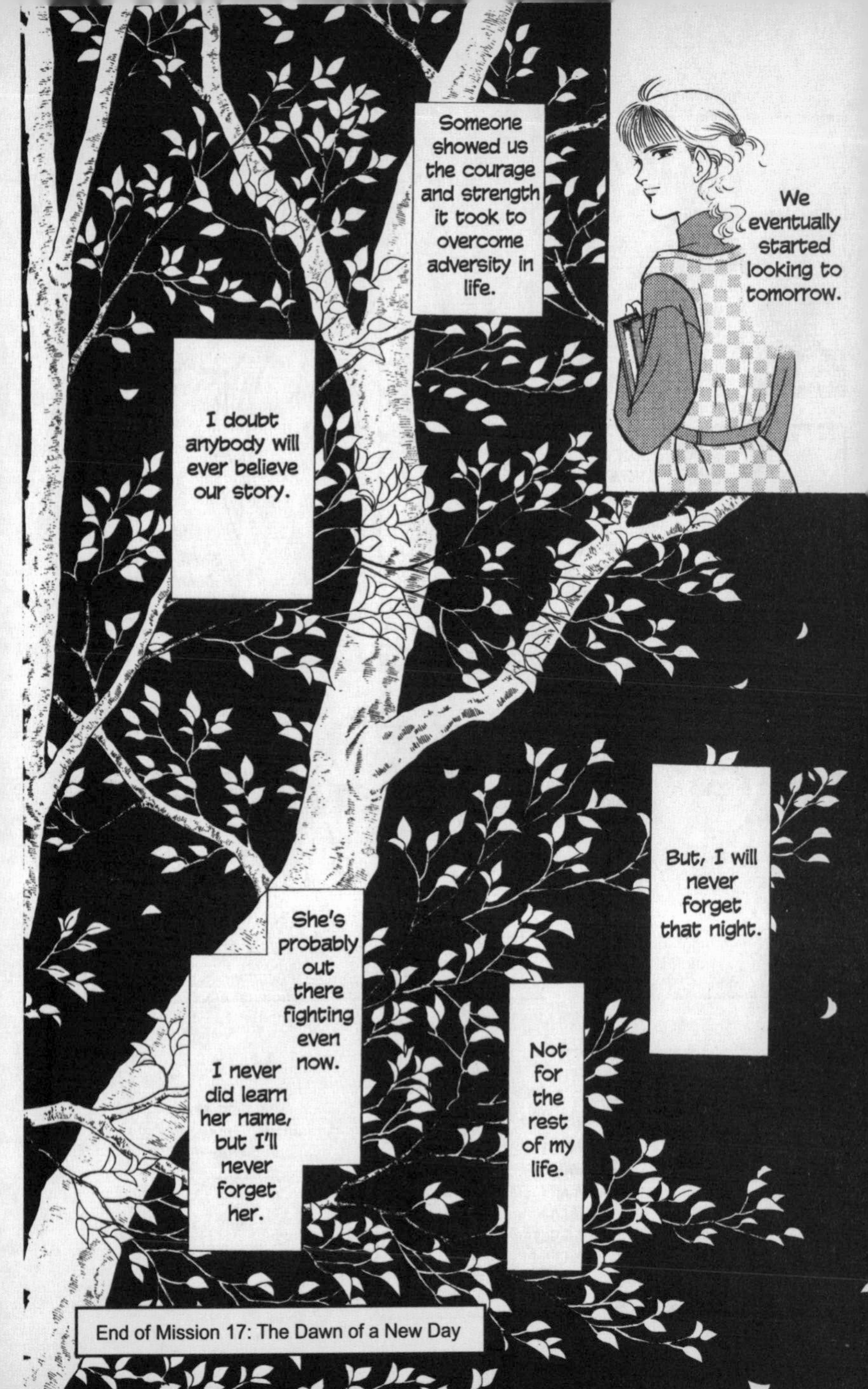
We eventually started looking to tomorrow.
Someone showed us the courage and strength it took to overcome adversity in life.
I doubt anybody will ever believe our story.
But, I will never forget that night.
Not for the rest of my life.
She's probably out there fighting even now.
I never did learn her name, but I'll never forget her.
End of Mission 17: The Dawn of a New Day

UB

Mission 18: The Forest of Dreams
I see the forest in my dreams.
It's on the edge where reality meets fantasy.
In it, wild but fantastic creatures roam free.
The forest does exist.
It invites us--lures us--into a world of fantasy.

9番目のムサシ
Mission 18: The Forest of Dreams

The dreams become real for an instant sometimes.
At the time, I was always daydreaming about the forest.
About the woods surrounding Grandma's house where I live when I was a kid.
About the trees I used to climb.
About the morning mist hanging over the lake.
About the creek where my dad and I used to go fishing for trout.
I have nothing but good memories of that place. It was the one spot I felt at ease.
ASAMI!
HEY, ASAMI!

STOP DAY-DREAMING AND HELP.
THERE'S A LOT TO DO HERE.
Huh?
What?
TALK ABOUT BEING RESERVED.
IF HE HATES IT HERE, WHY'D HE EVEN COME?
SO HE KNOWS HOW TO ROUGH IT. BIG DEAL.

I'M SURPRISED ASAMI ACTUALLY DID COME.
OF ALL THE FROSTIES, HE'S THE ONLY GUY THAT SHOWED.
SOMEBODY SAID HE GREW UP IN THE STATES.
OH. MAYBE THAT'S WHY HE ACTS LIKE HE'S MORE "MATURE."
HE CAN BE DOWNRIGHT STUCK-UP AT TIMES.
YEAH. WHAT'S WITH HIS HIGH AND MIGHTY ATTITUDE? HE'S JAPANESE--JUST LIKE US.
JOLT
OH...UM... HEY, ASAMI.
THANKS FOR BRINGING THE ROPE, DUDE.
Oops
WE WERE JUST TALKING ABOUT YOU. WE DIDN'T THINK YOU'D COME.
I MEAN, NO ONE FORCED YOU TO.

THE ONLY REASON WE'RE HERE IS BECAUSE OF THE GIRLS.
HA HA HA HA
IS THAT WHY YOU'RE HERE, TOO?
I DON'T PLAY CHILDREN'S GAMES.
INCIDENT-ALLY, MY GRAND-MOTHER'S WHITE.
SO, I'M NOT COMPLETELY JAPANESE.
THE GUY HEARD EVERY BIT OF IT.
THAT MUST'VE TEED HIM OFF BIG TIME.
THE GUY'S ALWAYS SO SERIOUS.
HE'S BEEN THAT WAY SINCE FIRST YEAR.
MAYBE HE'S, LIKE, MATURE BEYOND HIS YEARS, YA KNOW?
GOTTEN TO KNOW THE LADIES, IF YOU CATCH MY DRIFT.
AWESOME!
......
......
Those idiots.

It's too packed here. And, everyone's so narrow-minded. I'll never get used to this place.
RIPPLE RIPPLE
It's not as if I hate this country.
If you've got something to say, say it.
I really hate the way everyone pretends to be polite here.
SPLASH
It feels like something's missing.
Grandma... ...there's nowhere where I can really be myself.
Nowhere like that huge forest where every day was something special.
OH WOW
DID YOU KNOW? THERE'S A GUY IN THE NEXT CAMP WHO'S DROP DEAD GORGEOUS.
LET'S GO AND LOOK.
Kid's stuff.

YOU KNOW ABOUT THAT, RIGHT?
A HELICOPTER CRASHED A MONTH AGO IN THESE WOODS?
EVERYONE WAS KILLED INSTANTLY. BODY PARTS EVERYWHERE. STILL HAVEN'T FOUND ALL OF THEM.
AND THEN...
IT BEGAN...
WHERE IS MY HEAD?
WAUUUGH!
UM...HOW COME THERE ARE ONLY GUYS HERE?
WHERE'RE THE GIRLS?
YOU DON'T KNOW?
THEY'RE ALL AT THE NEXT CAMP-SITE.
THERE'S SUPPOSED TO BE SOME GOOD-LOOKING GUY THERE.
WHAT? NO WAY!
THAT MEANS WE CAME HERE FOR NOTHING!
THAT'S WHAT PEOPLE KEEP SAYING.
THE GUY'S APPARENTLY CAMPING HERE BY HIMSELF.
HEY.
HAVE ANY OF YOU SEEN MY SKETCH-BOOK?
THE ONE WITH THE GREEN COVER?
OH, THAT. IT WAS LEFT LYING AROUND IN THE TENT SO I PUT IT WITH THE OTHER JUNK.

THANKS.

I DIDN'T KNOW YOU WERE INTO DRAWING.

......

I'M NOT.

IT'S AN *EVIL* SKETCHBOOK.

PEOPLE WHO TOUCH IT BECOME CURSED, SO I WAS GOING TO THROW IT AWAY IN THE FOREST.

WAAUGH

No way! I touched it! I'm cursed!

Me, too!

Cursed with what?!

IDIOTS.

OH MY GOSH

OHWOW

That's who they were talking about.

With the girls draped all over him, no wonder the guys have it in for him.
But, look how thin that guy is. What do the girls see in a toothpick like him?

WHATEVER. IT'S GOT NOTHING TO DO WITH ME.
Sketch
Book
I inherited my ability to draw from grandma.
"Rather than take a photo, draw it if it's worth remembering.
"That way, both your hands and eyes will help you remember."
I sketched all the places I loved as a kid.
EXCUSE ME. CAN YOU HELP ME?
WHO'S IN CHARGE HERE?
But, look at this.
I haven't drawn a single picture since I came here.
Huh? That's the guy.

What does he want? Is he gonna whine about the girls all over him?
OUR HIGH SCHOOL TEACHER.
HE'S BY THE BONFIRE.
THANKS.
Yeah, go and whine. It must be so tough, huh?
ANY TIME.
YOU'RE QUITE THE ARTIST.
THAT'S GREEN LAKE IN MINNESOTA, ISN'T IT?
IT'S VERY NICELY DONE.

What the--?
WHAT'S HIS NAME?
WHOSE?
OH.
ASAMI?
THE GUY FROM THE NEXT CAMP. YOU KNOW, THE GUY YOU'RE DROOLING OVER.
HE JUST WENT BY HERE, DIDN'T HE?
SHINO-HARA YUU?
DID HE MEAN YUU?
HE CAME BY TO SAY IT'S DANGEROUS IN THE WOODS ON THE OTHER SIDE OF THE CREEK.
REAL-LY?
Shinohara Yuu?
That's the first time I talked to Asami!
Me, too! That was unexpected!
A little lake way out in the boons. I can't believe somebody here actually knows it even exists.

NNNNNNNNN
Are the little boys and girls still sleeping? It's mornings like this that make camping great. These losers would never understand that.
I'll try to find a good spot to sketch.
It's him!
GURGLE—
GURGLE—
That's the guy from yesterday!
I thought he said it was dangerous on the other side.
SPLASH
Classic case of do-as-I-say-not-as-I-do.

CHEEP CHEEP
CHEEP
CHIRP CHIRP CHIRP
"Listen very carefully, my child.
"There are fairies in the woods that like to play tricks. They sometimes make people get lost, so you have to be careful."
"Fairies? Really? What are they like? Have you ever seen one, grandma?"
"I have indeed."
"It was amazing.
"You could almost say it was divine.
"It was that beautiful."

STATION
COLLECTION
It was as if time had stopped.
Everything was perfectly still.

I swear.
It was as if Yuu was there and not there at the same time!
Yuu was one with the forest.
It was *perfect*.
"Have you ever seen one, grandma?"
"I have indeed.
"It was amazing.
"It was that beautiful."
THUNK

......
RUSTLE
RUSTLE RUSTLE
RUSTLE

RUSTLE RUSTLE RUSTLE
What am I doing? Why am I running?
I haven't done anything wrong, so why am I running?
HUFF
HUFF
HUF
OH, THERE YOU ARE.
EVERY-ONE'S ALREADY FINISHED BREAKFAST.
WE SAVED SOME FOR YOU, THOUGH.
NO THANKS. I'M NOT FEELING SO HOT.
FLAP
YOU ALL RIGHT?
THUMP THUMP
THUMP THUMP
I wish my heart would stop thumping!
What's all this about?

BUT, ACTUALLY, I'M LOOKING FOR SOMEONE NAMED ASAMI.
THANKS FOR THE WARNING. I TOLD EVERYONE LAST NIGHT.
OH WOW
IT'S SHINO-HARA!
ASAMI? HE'S RESTING AS HE'S NOT FEELING WELL.
GREAT.
JOLT
Sketch Book
THANKS FOR BRINGING IT.
HE DROPPED IT OVER THERE.
THEN CAN YOU GIVE THIS TO HIM?
THANKS AGAIN.
SURE.

......
THE GUY FROM THE NEXT CAMP BROUGHT THIS BY. IT IS YOURS, RIGHT?
THANK HIM LATER, WILL YOU?
OH. YOU'RE UP. I THOUGHT YOU WERE FEELING SICK.
I'm feeling a little more in control now.
But, for some reason, I'm also feeling pretty annoyed.
THUNK
Why'd I run?
The guy was a scrawny twig.
I could've taken him with one hand.
HEY, DUDE. IT'S YOUR OWN BUSINESS TO BE PISSED, BUT I DON'T WANNA FIND FINGERS FLOATING IN MY SOUP.
GLARE
OOH. SCARY.
WHAT'S EATIN' HIM? NOTHING USUALLY PHASES HIM.
HEY, IT'S--

I can understand trying to keep out those noisy pukes.
But, I don't like being considered one of them.
Not in the least!
THUNK
Why was he even there to begin with?
He's out there sitting pretty while he tells us not to.
YOU'D BETTER TAKE IT EASY BEFORE YOU CUT YOURSELF.
JOLT
YOU'RE ASAMI, RIGHT?
DID YOU GET YOUR SKETCH-BOOK BACK?
IF YOU DON'T MIND.
UM... ER...
YEAH... I DID.
THUMP THUMP
THUMP THUMP
Calm down. Calm down!

WHAT WERE YOU DOING OUT THERE THIS MORNING?
WHAT?
NOTHING REALLY.
I WAS OUT TAKING A WALK.
I SEE.
I WOULDN'T GO THERE IF I WERE YOU.
WHAT DO YOU MEAN?! I DO WHAT I--
THERE ARE SPOOKS.
SAY WHAT?
YOU DO KNOW A HELICOPTER CRASHED THERE LAST MONTH.
GHOULS HAVE BEEN OUT EVER SINCE.
ORDINARY PEOPLE WILL GET INTO TROUBLE IF THEY GO THERE.
THAT MEANS YOU, TOO.
I'D STAY AWAY FROM--
SLAP

HEY! STOP MESSING AROUND!
YOU THINK I'M JUST SOME LITTLE KID?
AND WHAT DO YOU MEAN BY "ORDINARY?!" DOES THAT MAKE YOU "SPECIAL?!"
I'M NOT AS NAÏVE AS YOU THINK!!
HEY NOW.
A FIGHT?
AND, IF IT AIN'T ROMEO.
YOU GOTTA PROBLEM WITH ONE OF OUR MATES?
GET LOST! YOU IDIOTS STAY OUT OF THIS!

SAY WHAT?!
GRRR
WHY DON'T YOU TAKE A HIKE? IT'S HIM WE WANT, NOT YOU!
YOU'RE SO TOUGH WHEN YOU'RE AROUND YOUR BUDDIES.
BUT, YOU SURE WHINE LIKE A WOMAN WHEN YOU'RE ALONE!
YOU MOUTHY LITTLE --!
CAN'T FIGURE OUT WHY THE GIRLS DON'T LIKE YOU? IT'S THAT PERSON-ALITY AND FACE OF YOURS!
TAKE A LOOK IN THE MIRROR BEFORE YOU CRITI-CIZE OTHERS.
YOU'RE GONNA PAY FOR THAT!
WHAM

THERE.
FEELING BETTER?
YOU DID IT NOW.
HE AIN'T MY FRIEND!
FRIENDS SHOULDN'T FIGHT.
BESIDES, I THOUGHT YOU WANTED ME.
......
AH... OOPS...
I BELIEVE THAT SETTLES YOUR SCORE, TOO.
YOU, TOO.
SPIN
......
WHAT-EVER.

YEAH, YEAH! I HEARD YOU ALREADY!
AND, STAY AWAY FROM THE FOREST. IT REALLY IS DANGEROUS.
......
GOOD.
What is it with him? Huh? Huh?
The guy thinks he's so cool.
He thinks he saved my hide. Whatever!
He should've stayed out of it if he thinks fighting is so uncool.
He got hit by that idiot.
YOU FEELING SICK AGAIN?
Some-thing must be wrong with me.
Why am I getting so worked up over some guy I've just met?
Why all this rage?
What's eating away at me?

I stopped going to the forest after that.
Shinohara wasn't around after that.
I did, however, get more depressed with every passing day.
I just wanted to get away from that place as fast as I could.
Something must be wrong with me.
It's not him I want to kill.
It's the guy that hit him.
Do I hate him that much?
Nah. It's not that.
LET'S GO OUT WITH A BANG!
LOOK AT IT GO!
CRANK UP THE MUSIC!
IT'S RIPPING NOW!

YOU DON'T LOOK LIKE A HAPPY CAMPER.
HATANO AND THEM FEEL PRETTY BAD ABOUT IT, SO LET IT GO. ALL RIGHT?
Hatano? Who's Hatano? Oh. So that's his name.
COME ON. IT'S THE LAST NIGHT. TRY TO ENJOY YOURSELF, OKAY?
I'd already forgotten about that.
The dream the forest showed me. A summer day's dream.
What do people call this sort of thing?
It's the same as when I was really young. Just one second, but it was seared into my memory.
That's what it seems like.
Sketch Book
I shouldn't have gotten all defensive like that.
FLASH
I should've just made friends with

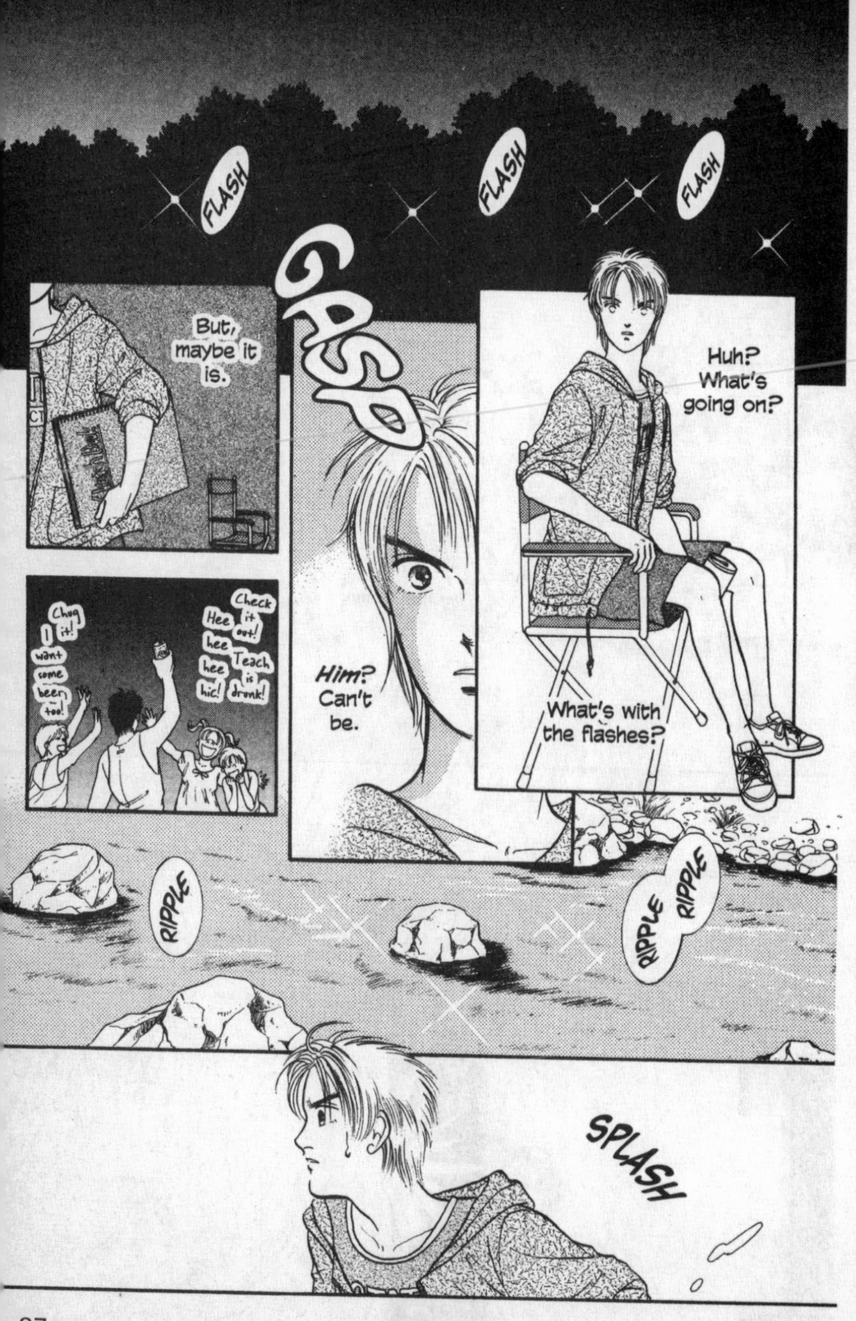
FLASH
FLASH
FLASH
GASP
Huh? What's going on?
What's with the flashes?
Him? Can't be.
But, maybe it is.
Check it out! Teach is drunk!
Hee hee hee hic!
Chug it!
I want some beer, too!
RIPPLE
RIPPLE
RIPPLE
SPLASH

If it's him, I'm gonna apologize to him *properly*.
The guy seems cool enough.
I'll talk to him straight up.
About Green Lake. About things in general.
He'd be a good friend.
I'm fairly sure...
SQUISH
...he's gonna be *there*.
There he is!

Huh?!
What the--?! Guns?! This can't be right!
I think I'm still in Japan, so what are they doin' with guns?
The police! I've gotta call the police!
<HEY! I FOUND ANOTHER ONE!>

BUSTED!
RUSTLE
TSK
<ANOTHER ONE?*>
<JUST ANOTHER KID CAMPING.>
<OF ALL THE STUPID PLACES TO GO DOWN, THE HELICOPTER HAD TO CRASH HERE.>
WUMP
<*GO JOIN YOUR PAL!>

<*BRACKETS INDICATE THEY ARE SPEAKING ENGLISH>

DIDN'T I TELL YOU *NOT* TO COME HERE?
WELL, YEAH, BUT...
WHAT DO THEY WANT? WHO ARE THEY?
THEY SAID SOMETHING ABOUT A HELICOPTER.
SH! DON'T LET THEM KNOW YOU UNDERSTAND ENGLISH.
<AIN'T THE BOSS HERE YET?>
<HE'S ON HIS WAY.>
<SO, THEY'RE FINALLY GONNA COMPLETE THE DEAL.>
<THE OTHER GUY'S CHOPPER GOING DOWN HERE WAS COMPLETELY UNEXPECTED.>
<GOOD THING WE HAD A TRANSMITTER IN WITH THE BAGS. I DON'T EVEN WANNA THINK ABOUT WHAT WE'D BE DOING RIGHT NOW IF IT WEREN'T FOR THAT.>
<BUT, WHY DO THE DEAL HERE?>
<THE GOODS BEING WHAT THEY ARE, THE BOSS FIGURED IT'D BE SAFER IF IT WERE LEFT UNTOUCHED.>
<NO SENSE IN RECOVERING THEM AND GETTING INTO MORE PROBLEMS, YOU KNOW?>

<I CAN'T BELIEVE SOME OF THE TECH STUFF THIS COUNTRY COOKS UP.>
<CAN YOU BELIEVE IT? THE WORLD'S FASTEST JET ENGINE? EVEN FASTER THAN A MISSILE?>
<THE INVENTOR MEANT IT FOR PEACEFUL PURPOSES. BUT, HEY, WHEN DOES THE MILITARY ***NOT*** WANT SOMETHING LIKE THAT?>
<THAT'S WHY THE BOSS IS WORRIED.>
<HE DOESN'T TRUST THE SELLER. CAN'T BLAME HIM THOUGH.>
<THE GUY WAS SMART ENOUGH TO STEAL THE PLANS, BUT HE LOST THEM IN THE MOUNTAINS.>
<THE BOSS WANTS TO MAKE A KILLING--OR TWO.>
<IT'S STILL IN THE DEVELOPMENT STAGE, BUT GOVERNMENTS ARE ALREADY LINING UP TO BUY IT.>
THERE IS SOME SERIOUS STUFF GOING DOWN.
UH-HUH.
LIKE, THESE GUYS ARE INTERNATIONAL CRIMINALS OR SOMETHING.
I KNOW.
THEN HOW CAN YOU BE SO CALM?
DOESN'T ANYONE HERE TAKE THIS SORT OF STUFF SERIOUSLY?
<HEY! SHUT UP!>
<YO, THE BOSS IS HERE.>

<AH, MR. MATSUDA. DO YOU HAVE WHAT WE WANT?>

<YES. WE'VE JUST RECOVERED THEM.>

<AS PER YOUR REQUEST.>

<SORRY FOR THE INCONVENIENCE, BUT I DIDN'T THINK IT WOULD BE A GOOD IDEA TO TRY MOVING THEM AGAIN.>

<I CAN UNDERSTAND YOUR CONCERN, BUT WE HAD A VERY DIFFICULT TIME IN STEALING THEM IN THE FIRST PLACE.>
<I'M SURE YOU DID.>
<YOU CAME OUT HERE TO MAKE OUT.>
<BUT, IT ENDED UP LIKE THIS.>
<NOT YOUR LUCKY DAY, KIDS.>
Say what?
<DON'T MATTER WHERE YOU'RE FROM. YOU ALL HAVE THE SAME THING IN MIND.>
What?
<HEY, WAS THIS GONNA BE YOUR FIRST TIME WITH A GIRL?>
<MAYBE WE'LL LET YOU SEE HEAVEN BEFORE WE SEND YOU TO HELL.>
HAR HAR HAR
<YOU WANTED TO PLAY WITH FIRE, BUT YOU GOT BURNED IN THE WRONG WAY, KID.>
HEY, THESE BOZOS THINK YOU'RE A CHICK!
YOU GONNA LET THAT STAND?!

......
FIX?
Why?
WELL, BECAUSE...
BE-BE-BECAUSE... NO.
NO WAY!
<WHAT?>
CLICK
THERE ARE SEVERAL THINGS THAT NEED TO BE FIXED, ACTUALLY.
ONE IN PARTICULAR, THOUGH.

THE PART ABOUT US DYING.
<HEY! WHEN DID SHE GET UNTIED?!>
GRIP
PAFF
WAUGH!
THOK

CLICK
PTUI
AIIEEEE!
SHISH
TOK

RUSTLE
RUSTLE RUSTLE
HIDE HERE UNTIL THIS IS OVER.
UNDER-STAND?
RUSTLE
HEY, WHERE'RE YOU GOING?
HEY!
What was all that?
Just who is she?

BLAM
BLAM
RAT-TAT-TAT-TAT
BLAM
BSH
BSH
URK!
<WHO IS? WHO'S SHOOTING AT US?>
<I DON'T KNOW, BUT WE HAVE TO GET OUT OF HERE!>
<IT'S NO GOOD.>
<WE CAN'T DO ANYTHING! HE'S TOO GOOD!>

BSH
BSH
BSH
HEE HEE
HEE
BSH
GZZZ
<THE END.>

FWOOOSSH
WAUGH!
POP
<THE PLANS!>
<MY PLANS!>
<IT'S BEST YOU GIVE IT UP..>
<IT'S OVER..>

<LET ME DOWN! OR ELSE, YOU'LL PAY DEARLY!>
<DO YOU KNOW WHO I AM?>
<YOU'RE THAT KID.>
<YOU? YOU DID THIS?>
<WE DO IN FACT, MR. GORDON. YOU'RE AN ARMS DEALER.>
<WE'RE QUITE WILLING TO FIGHT.>
<THAT IS OF COURSE IF YOU WANT TO GO UP AGAINST *ULTIMATE BLUE*.>
<ULTIMATE...>
<...BLUE?>

I TOLD YOU IT WAS DANGER-OUS.
TATIC
OLLECT
IT'S ALL RIGHT NOW, THOUGH.
THEY'RE YOUR WOODS AGAIN.

I think I understand now, grandma.
I think I know why you remember certain places.
You remember them because of the people you were with.
I swear, that forest looked brilliant.
YO, LONG TIME, TAKERU.
HOW WAS THE CAMPING?
IT MUST HAVE TOTALLY SUCKED WITH THOSE LITTLE KIDS.
LEAVE ME ALONE.
GOOD MORNING TO YOU, TOO.
SOME-THING HAPPEN?
Come to think of it, maybe it was love.

What a sight.
The way she looked in the morning light...man.
I think I was in love.
What else would explain why I can't forget her?
I just never realized it because I thought she was a guy.
Not that I can do anything about it.
She ain't ordinary.
She's real, and yet she's not.
That's just the way she is.
I'll just pretend I tripped out in the forest.
That was how my summer ended.
Or, so I thought.
HUH?
WHAT'S THAT?
I DUNNO. IT WAS CAUGHT IN MY SKETCHBOOK.
WHAT ARE THESE WEIRD NUMBERS AND STUFF?

I SWEAR...
IT LOOKS LIKE...
A BLUE-PRINT.
RATTLE
SIT DOWN, PLEASE!
WE HAVE A NEW STUDENT.
Summer ended all right.
But, it wasn't the end.
It was just the beginning for me--or rather, us.
End of Mission 18: The Forest of Dreams

Mission 19: Omega - Part 1

I had a hard time believing it was real.

Yuu was always in those woods.

Right off the bat, I knew Yuu was something special.

I thought it was game over when a bunch of heavies caught us.

That's when the real Yuu showed.

I thought I was in a dream.

Yuu took out these mercenaries like it was nothing. Didn't need any help, either. But, that was nothing compared to the real surprise.

Yuu was a *girl*.

YOU GOT TAKEN FOR A RIDE!
MAYBE YOU WERE FOOLED BY SOME GUYS PLAYING PAINTBALL OR SOMETHING.
OR ELSE YOU JUST DREAMT IT ALL UP.
YOU'RE ASKING ME TO BELIEVE THAT STORY?
MERCENARIES? SHOOTING? *IN JAPAN?* YEAH, RIGHT!

NO, I DIDN'T!
RATTLE
LOOK! HERE'S THE *PROOF!*

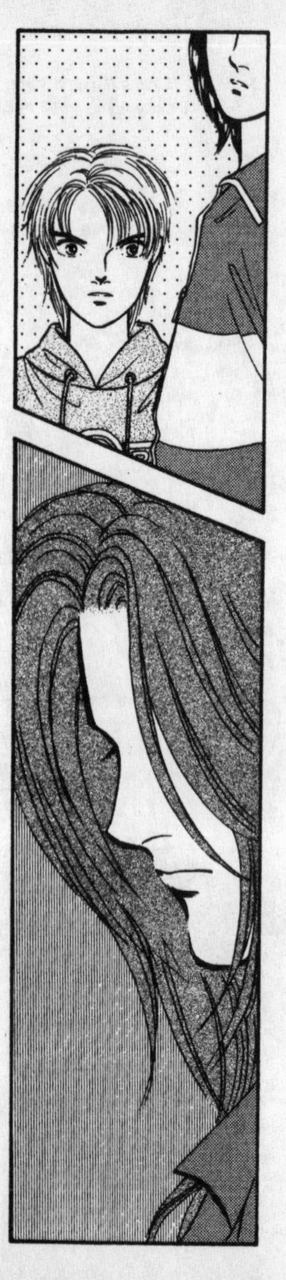

9番目のムサシ
ばんめ
Mission 19: Omega - Part 1

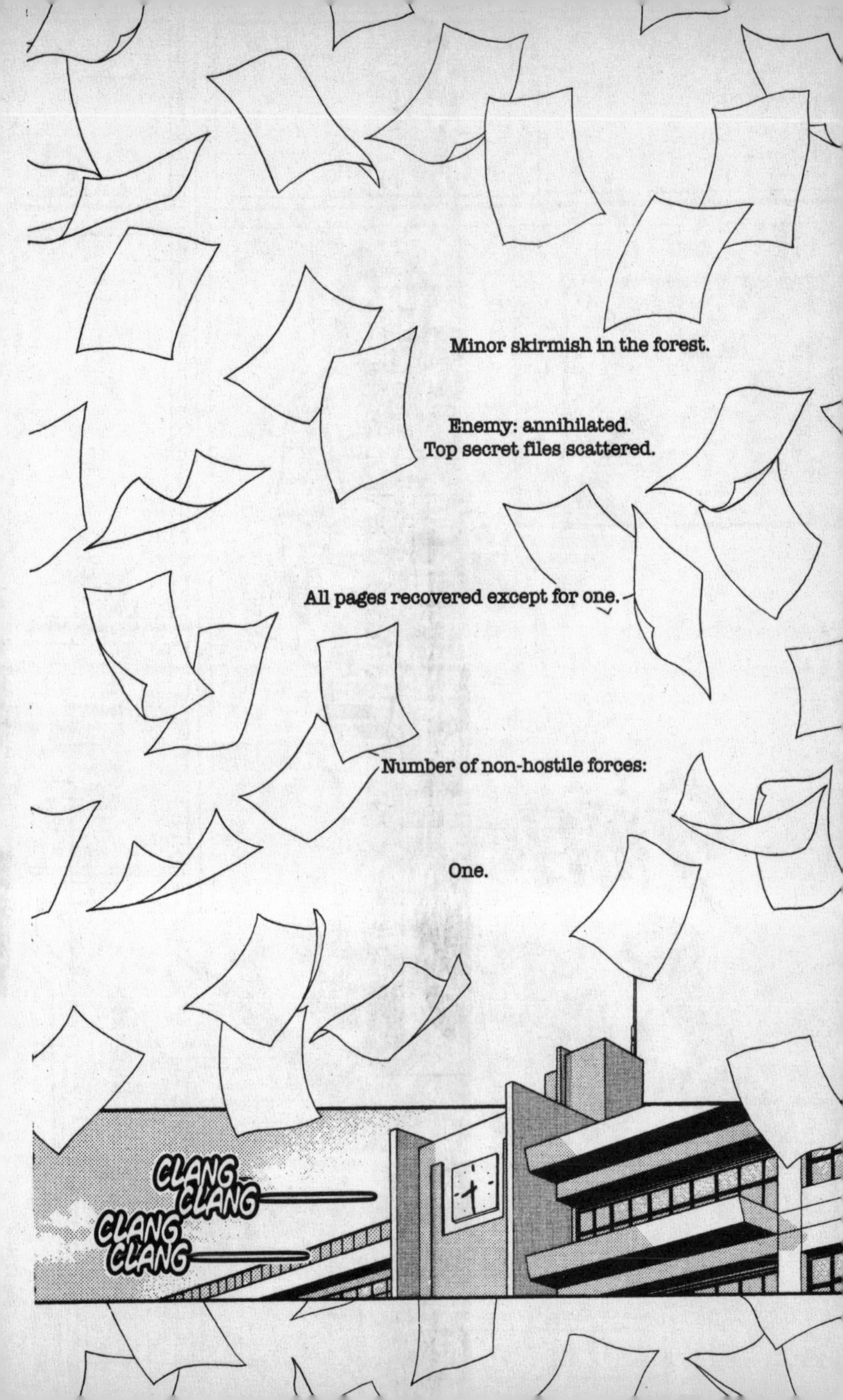
Minor skirmish in the forest.
Enemy: annihilated.
Top secret files scattered.
All pages recovered except for one.
Number of non-hostile forces:
One.
CLANG CLANG
CLANG CLANG

<...AS WELL AS THE LARGE KITCHEN ON THE GROUND FLOOR.>
<OVER THE YEARS, THEY FURNISHED THE ROOMS IN WAYS THAT REFLECTED...>
<...A STYLISH SENSE OF IMAGINATION AND WIT.>
THANK YOU.
MS. SHINOHARA, CONTINUE PLEASE.
OKAY.
<SMITH TOOK THE SAME ATTITUDE WITH...>
WHY ARE THE GIRLS ACTING LIKE THAT?!
SHINOHARA'S A GIRL!
SURE DON'T LOOK IT.
SORRY, MA'AM. I DON'T KNOW HOW TO READ THE REST.

OH.
WELL, THAT WAS FINE.
CLAT
You liar!
You lying ...!
Your English is *perfect*.
Why are you trying to hide it?
Just what are you trying to pull?
GASP
I'M SO SORRY! IT WAS A TERRIBLE PASS!
NO, NO. IT WAS MY FAULT. I'M ALL THUMBS.
I'LL GET IT.
It's an act. It's a total act!
She's doing it on purpose.
HEY! HURRY UP AND PASS THE BALL!

SHE'S NOTHING LIKE WHAT YOU SAID.
YOU SAID HER ENGLISH WAS PERFECT.
AND THAT SHE HAD UNREAL REFLEXES.
LOOKS TOTALLY NORMAL TO ME.
THE ONLY THING UNUSUAL ABOUT HER IS SHE LOOKS LIKE A GUY.
DUDE, SHUT UP!
THAT'S NOT THE *REAL* SHINO-HARA.
I'M TELLING YOU, DUDE, SHE'S ***UNREAL***.
SHE'S PUTTING ON AN ACT.
......
SURE. WHAT-EVER.

WELL, OF COURSE, I'M PRETENDING TO A CERTAIN DEGREE.
I DON'T WANT TO STAND OUT.
WHAT? SO THAT NOBODY WILL FIGURE OUT WHO YOU REALLY ARE?
Tee hee
NOBODY WILL, EVEN WITHOUT THE PRETENDING.
I DON'T WANT TO INVITE HOSTILITY BY STANDING OUT.
I TRY TO AVOID PROBLEMS WITH CIVILIANS.
......
True enough. You're anything but ordinary.
I thought people like you didn't exist. Who did you say you worked for? U.B.? V.?
COULD WE HAVE THAT PAGE BACK?
IT WOULD SOLVE OUR MUTUAL PROBLEMS.
I TOLD YOU. I DON'T KNOW WHERE IT IS!

SO, JUST LEAVE ME ALONE! ALL RIGHT?!
WHY WOULD I HAVE SOMETHING LIKE THAT ANYWAY?!
THEN WHAT DID YOU HIDE SO QUICKLY EARLIER?
JOLT
YOU MAY NOT UNDER-STAND IT.
BUT, FOR THE PEOPLE WHO CAN, THAT ONE PAGE SPEAKS VOLUMES.
WHY WON'T YOU GIVE IT BACK?
I DON'T KNOW WHAT YOU'RE TALKING ABOUT!
THAT SHEET YOU SAW WAS A BAD DRAWING I RIPPED OUT OF MY SKETCH-BOOK!
YOU MUST HAVE NOTHING BETTER TO DO.
YOU'RE UNDER-COVER, LOOKING FOR JUST A SINGLE PAGE OF SOMETHING?
YES. THAT IS THE *PRIMARY* OBJECTIVE.

WE TOOK OUT THE MAIN FORCE, BUT SOME OF THEM ARE STILL AT LARGE.
THEY'RE DESPERATELY LOOKING FOR THEIR BOSS. IN ALL LIKELIHOOD, THEY DON'T KNOW WHAT HAPPENED.
THAT SAID, THE REMNANTS OF THAT GROUP MAY SHOW UP HERE-- HOWEVER UNLIKELY.
THEY'RE MOSTLY LOW-LEVEL, SO THERE'S NOTHING TO WORRY ABOUT.
NONETHELESS, IT'S ALSO MY JOB TO PROTECT YOU UNTIL MY TEAM ROUNDS THEM UP.
I DON'T NEED NO GIRL PROTECTING ME, THANK YOU!
......
Hee hee
WHAT?! WHAT'S SO FUNNY?!
OH. SORRY. I WASN'T LAUGHING AT YOU.
I JUST REMEM-BERED A TIME TO SIMILAR THIS.

I ONCE HAD TO PROTECT SOMEONE, LIKE I'M DOING NOW.
HE'S ABOUT YOUR AGE.
HE'S REALLY SWEET.
I WAS JUST WONDERING HOW HE WAS DOING.
I HOPE HE'S DOING ALL RIGHT.
SPIN
ASAMI.
Just who is *he*?!
What's with that face?!
I *DON'T* KNOW ANYTHING ABOUT ANY PLANS, OKAY?
SO, GO LOOK ELSEWHERE!
HEY, LOVEBIRDS.

PAT
KANAME! WHAT ARE YOU DOING?!
WHOOSH
ARE YOU NUTS, YOU SICK PIG?! DON'T FEEL HER UP LIKE THAT!
SHE'S NOT PACKIN'.
I'M SORRY TO TELL YA, BUD. SHE AIN'T NO--
HI, SHINO-HARA.
WE USE A DIFFERENT LOCKER ROOM WHEN P.E. IS OUTSIDE. YOU PROBABLY DIDN'T KNOW THAT, SO WE'LL TAKE YOU THERE.
REALLY? THANKS A LOT.
OOHHH
IT'S NOTHING.

MUMBLE MUMBLE
......
WHY DID YOU LIE TO HER?
ABOUT WHAT?
THAT SHEET.
T'S ALL BOUT THE HEET THAT WAS AUGHT IN YOUR KETCH-BOOK, RIGHT?
WHY DID OU TELL ER YOU DIDN'T NOW?
IT AIN'T GOT NOTHING TO DO WITH YOU.
ADMIT IT. *YOU LIKE HER.*
WHAT?
YOU REALLY DO BELIEVE THAT FANTASY OF YOURS, DON'T YOU?
YOU ALSO BELIEVE SHE'S GONNA SPLIT THE SECOND SHE GETS THAT PAGE BACK.

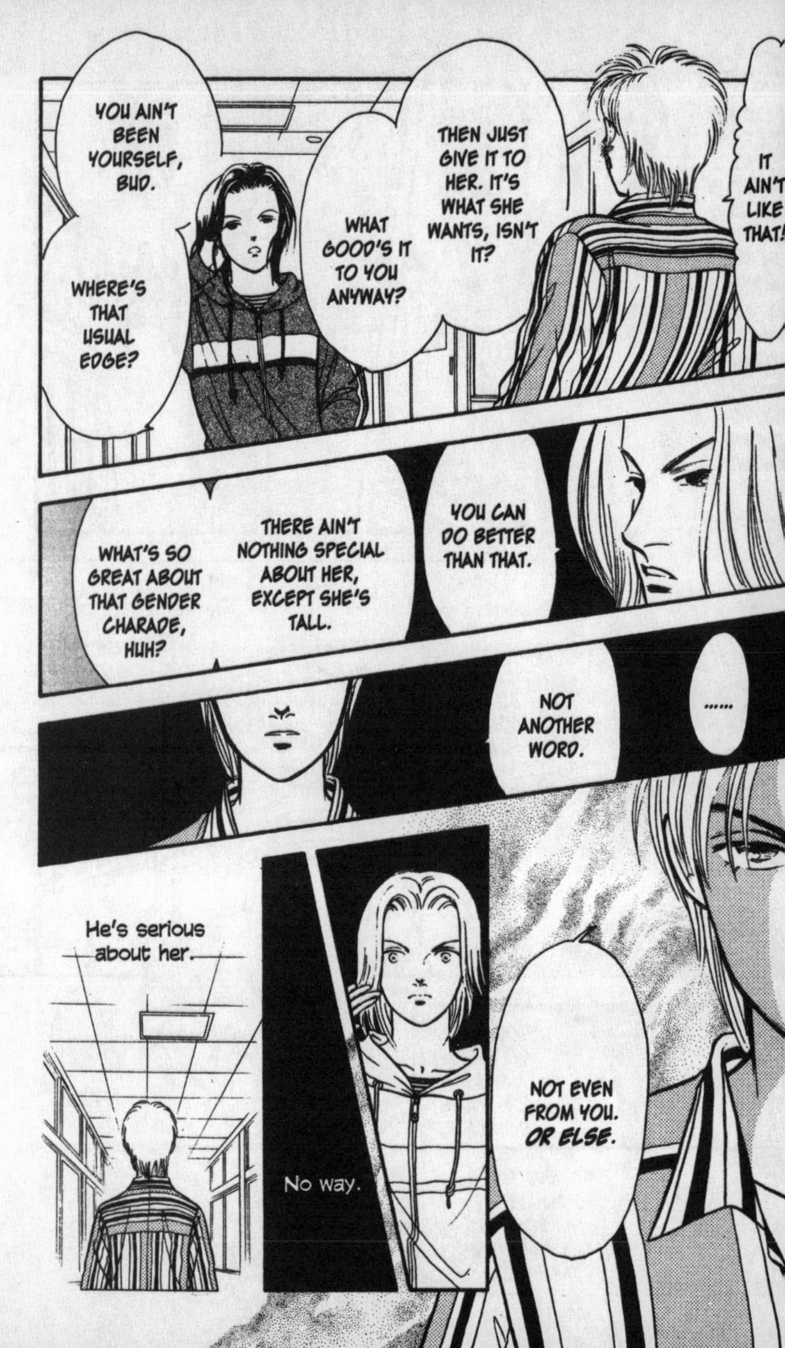
IT AIN'T LIKE THAT!
THEN JUST GIVE IT TO HER. IT'S WHAT SHE WANTS, ISN'T IT?
WHAT GOOD'S IT TO YOU ANYWAY?
YOU AIN'T BEEN YOURSELF, BUD.
WHERE'S THAT USUAL EDGE?
YOU CAN DO BETTER THAN THAT.
THERE AIN'T NOTHING SPECIAL ABOUT HER, EXCEPT SHE'S TALL.
WHAT'S SO GREAT ABOUT THAT GENDER CHARADE, HUH?
......
NOT ANOTHER WORD.
NOT EVEN FROM YOU. *OR ELSE.*
No way.
He's serious about her.

THE OMEGA CLUB?
IS THAT WHAT ASAMI'S IN?
YEAH.
WITH THAT NAKAMURA KANAME.
I'D STAY AWAY FROM THEM.
THEY'RE TOTAL SNAKES.
THEY'RE SO CONDESCEND-ING. THEY THINK THEY'RE SPECIAL.
AYBE IT AN'T BE ELPED.
ONLY THE REALLY SMART OR MPORTANT KIDS CAN GET IN.
I SEE.
ANYWAY, THEY'RE TOTAL NERDS.
HEY. WHAT'S THAT?
IT DOESN'T LOOK LIKE A SPORTS BRA. IT LOOKS... HARD.
ISN'T IT CONSTRICT-ING?
IT'S LIKE ONE.
I'M USED TO IT.
I WEAR IT ALL THE TIME.

THUNK

I KNEW THOSE THREE WOULDN'T SHOW.

IT'S PRETTY BORING WITH JUST THE TWO OF US.

THAT'S JUST THE WAY IT IS. THEY ALWAYS COME AND GO AS THEY PLEASE.

THEY DON'T THINK ANYTHING OF SCHOOL.

MUST BE GREAT BEING SO SMART YOU CAN SKIP OUT ALL THE TIME.

WE GOT OURS. THEY GOT THEIRS. GOOD ENOUGH, I SAY.

WHAT DO YOU WANNA DO NOW? WANNA GO OUT?
NAH. I'M GOING STRAIGHT HOME.
I'VE GOTTA GO BY THE HOSPITAL.
WHAT? MAKOTO?
HOW'S YOUR BROTHER DOIN' THESE DAYS?
SO SO, I GUESS.
SOME DAYS HE'S GOOD. SOME DAYS HE'S NOT SO GOOD.
CONGENITAL HEART PROBLEM, RIGHT?
ARE THEY GONNA OPER-ATE?
NOT YET.
MY OLD MAN CAN'T DECIDE. THE DOC REALLY CAN'T SAY ONE WAY OR THE OTHER.
MY BRO' HAS A LESS THAN FIFTY-FIFTY CHANCE OF SURVIVING.
BESIDES, HE'S TOO WEAK TO UNDERGO AN OPERATION.
HEAVY.
I FEEL SORRY FOR THE LITTLE GUY.
HUH?

WHO DO WE HAVE HERE? IT'S ASAMI.
COMING BACK FROM THAT LITTLE CLUB OF YOURS?
DID YOU DISCUSS HOW TO PUT A LID ON THAT STUCK-UP TRAP OF YOURS? NOW THAT WOULD HAVE BEEN WORTHWHILE.
I'D WORRY MORE ABOUT HOW MUCH OF AN IDIOT YOU ARE.
YOU'RE ONLY HERE 'CAUSE YOUR PARENTS ARE RICH. YOU'RE NOWHERE NEAR SMART ENOUGH.
YOUR SKULL'S PRETTY THICK, BUT I THINK I CAN TEACH YOU A THING OR TWO.

IF YOU WANT ANY HELP, JUST SAY THE WORD.
IT'LL COST YOU, THOUGH.
UCHIDA DOESN'T GIVE IT A REST, DOES HE?
MAYBE HE'S BORED.
HE KEEPS AT YOU 'CAUSE YOU KEEP LAYIN' INTO HIM LIKE THAT.
I DON'T LIKE THAT DWEEB.
HE'S RETARDED, BUT THINKS HE'S THE MAN 'CAUSE HIS DAD'S A POLITICIAN.
YOU'RE NOT MUCH DIFFERENT. YOUR OLD MAN'S A FOREIGN MINISTRY BUREAU-CRAT.
UH-HUH. AND THAT'S WHY UCHIDA CAN'T TOUCH ME.
YOU'RE NEEDLING HIM 'CAUSE YOU'RE BORED, TOO.
YEAH. THAT OBVI-OUS?
I'm just being me.
THAT STUPID...
WHAT'S WRONG, DUDE?
HIM AGAIN?
THAT CON-CEITED JERK?

JUST ONCE, I'D LIKE TO WASTE THAT LITTLE TWERP!
SHOW HIM WHO'S REALLY BOSS.
WHO DO THOSE OMEGA GUYS THINK THEY ARE, ANYWAY? THEY THINK THEY'RE SO HOT.
DON'T MESS WITH THE OMEGAS.
THEY CAN MAKE LIFE MISER-ABLE FOR YOU LATER.
BUT, I'LL MAKE AN EXCEP-TION FOR ASAMI.
HE'S GONNA PAY.
BUT, HOW? HE'LL BE HARD TO GET AT.
I'M THINK-ING ABOUT IT.
LUCKILY, THE OTHER OMEGAS AIN'T HERE RIGHT NOW.
IF WE'RE GONNA DO HIM, WE DO HIM NOW.
I HAVE TO FIGURE OUT HOW TO GET HIM OUT INTO THE OPEN.
D. K.
JUST YOU WATCH.
I'M GONNA SETTLE SCORES *BIG TIME* WITH HIM.

RATTLE
......
HEY, MAKO-TO.
KANAME!

YOU BEEN GOOD?
HERE'S THE GAME I PROMISED YOU.
ALL RIGHT!
IT'S MAKO-TO'S BROTHER.
HEY, MOM.
YOU MADE IT.
HOW IS HE?
HE HAD A MINOR ATTACK THIS MORNING.
THE DOCTOR SAYS WE HAVE TO DECIDE SOON.
OH.

WHAT'S THE OLD MAN SAYING?
PLOP
HE'S NOT SURE.
MAKOTO COULD DIE DURING THE OPERATION.
THE DOCTOR SAYS HE'LL DO HIS BEST.
BUT, I AN'T...I ST DON'T KNOW.
C'MON, MOM.
HEY, BRO!
NO RUN-NING.
SHOW ME HOW TO PLAY THIS!
KEEP IT DOWN, BOYS.
SURE, MOM!

DING DING
DING DING
HEY, UCHI-DA.
LISTEN TO THIS, DUDE.
WHAT?
A WAY OF GETTING AT ASAMI.
I STARTED LOOKIN' INTO THE OMEGA GUYS, YEAH?
WELL, ONE OF EM'S ALWAYS WITH ASAMI--A GUY NAMED NAKAMURA.
APPARENT-LY, HIS YOUNGER BROTHER'S IN A *PUBLIC* HOSPITAL.
HE'S GOT SOMETHING BAD. IT GETS BETTER. KANAME'S PARENTS AIN'T RICH.
I THINK WE CAN USE THIS.
YOU'RE RIGHT. I THINK WE CAN.

WE'LL HIT HIM FROM THE SIDE...
HEY, SHUT UP.
SOME-ONE'S THERE.
HUH?
HEY! WE KNOW YOU'RE THERE!
WHAT WERE YOU DOIN'?
IT'S P.E.
THAT'S BULL, MAN. THERE'S NO ONE ELSE AROUND!
YOU WERE SPYIN' ON US!

I'M HERE EARLY TO GET THINGS READY.
I DIDN'T HEAR ANY-THING.
YEAH, RIGHT.
WE NEED TO BRING THE PAIN TO SHUT HIM UP.
HEH HEH...
STOP RIGHT THERE.
NOW WHAT?
YOU INTO BEATIN' WOMEN NOW?

HUH?
WHAT? A GIRL?
TODAY'S CO-ED P.E.
YOU'RE RIGHT.
LET'S GET OUT OF HERE.
HEY, SHINO.
HURRY UP AND GET EVERYTHING READY.
EVERY-ONE'S GONNA BE HERE SOON.
HEY, NAKA-MURA.
EVERY-ONE?
NOT GOOD.
WE GOTTA TALK. IT'S ABOUT *YOUR* BROTHER.

NAKA-
MURA?
TELL 'IM I GOT SICK AND WENT TO THE NURSE'S.
......
WHAT DO YOU WANT?

IF IT'S ALL THE SAME, WOULDN'T A HOSPITAL WITH THE LATEST AND GREATEST BE MORE REASSURING?
AND, YOU WON'T HAVE TO WORRY ABOUT THE BILLS. I CAN HAVE THEM TAKEN CARE OF.
THINK ABOUT IT. IT'S FOR FAMILY.
IS THAT ALL? I'M OUTTA HERE.
ASAMI.
I JUST WANT YOU TO CALL HIM.
DO THAT, AND I'LL GET THE BALL ROLLING.
SO, THAT'S WHAT THIS IS ALL ABOUT.

OBVIOUSLY, YOU THINK I'M NOTHIN'.
YOU THINK I'M GONNA SELL OUT A FRIEND JUST BECAUSE YOU BROUGHT UP MY FAMILY?
I AIN'T LIKE YOU SCUMBAGS.
REMEM-BER THIS.
I HATE NOTHING MORE THAN BEING PLAYED A FOOL-- BY A FOOL.
ESPECIALLY BY IDIOTS LIKE YOU WHO DON'T HAVE TWO BRAIN CELLS TO RUB TOGETHER.
CHILL OUT.
NAKAMURA, I THINK YOU SHOULD THINK THIS THROUGH.
MY OLD MAN'S PRETTY INFLUEN-TIAL.
I CAN EVEN HAVE YOUR BROTHER THROWN OUT OF THE HOSPITAL HE'S IN NOW.
OH YEAH?!
POW

"MY OLD MAN" THIS AND "MY OLD MAN" THAT.
YOU'RE OLD MAN'S AN IDIOT. HE'S AT THE BECK AND CALL OF A RETARD.
WHY DO I GET THE FEELING HE'S LIKE YOU--AN INSECURE NOBODY WHO HAS TO ACT BIG?
......
I DON'T THINK YOU UNDERSTAND YOUR PREDICA-MENT.
DO IT.
LET'S LEAVE IT AT THAT.

HEY, IT'S BUTCH.
GET LOST. THIS AIN'T GOT NOTHING TO DO WITH YOU.
I DON'T THINK THERE'S A NEED FOR ALL THIS YELLING.
SHUT UP, YOU BEE-YATCH!
HANG ON.
YOU'RE PRETTY GOOD LOOKING.
I DON'T WANT TO MESS UP THAT PRETTY FACE OF YOURS.
BUT, WE'RE ALSO INTO EQUAL RIGHTS HERE. GIRLS GET IT JUST AS BAD.
YEAH. GET OUTTA HERE.

WHAT ARE YOU STANDING AROUND HERE FOR? GET LOST!
IT'S MY PROBLEM, NOT YOURS!
IT ALL STARTED BECAUSE I GOT HERE TOO EARLY.
I'D BETTER DEAL WITH IT.
DEAL WITH IT?
HA HA HA HA HA
WHAT'S YOUR DEAL?
CAN'T YOU SEE WHAT'S GOING ON?
WHAT CAN YOU DO BY YOURSELF?
WHO SAID I WAS ALONE?
HUH?
I BROUGHT A FEW OF MY FRIENDS.

Mission 19: Omega - Part 2
HEY, WHAT HAPPENED TO YOUR FACE?
DID SOMEBODY HIT YOU? HUH?
JUST SHUT UP. I TRIPPED, OKAY?
TRIPPED?! YEAH, RIGHT! WHO'S THE JERK THAT DID IT?!
IT'S GOT NOTHIN' TO DO WITH YOU!
SO, QUIT BARKING, ALL RIGHT?!
WHAT DO YOU MEAN, IT'S GOT NOTHING TO DO WITH ME?! I THOUGHT WE WERE--
"FRIENDS?"
DEFINITELY UNCOOL, I'D SAY.

ON THE OTHER HAND, NOBODY LIKES A STUBBORN FRIEND.
......
WITH EVERY PASSING DAY, THAT SKULL OF YOURS KEEPS GETTIN' THICKER. YOU'LL BE A NEANDERTHAL IN NO TIME. MAYBE EVEN CRO-MAGNON.
SAY WHAT?
WORRY ABOUT YOUR-SELVES FOR A CHANGE.
KEEP DE-EVOLVING AT THE RATE YOU ARE, WE'RE GONNA BE IN THE SAME GRADE. THAT WOULD KILL ME.
WHY YOU LITTLE--!
LEAVE HIM ALONE.
WE ONLY WANT TO TALK TO KANAME.

Kaname?
IT'S GOT NOTHING TO DO WITH ME. LET'S GO.
THAT'S COLD, DUDE.
DID YOU THINK ABOUT WHAT I SAID?
WHAT ARE YOU GOONS TALKING ABOUT?
IT WAS YOU?
I DON'T KNOW WHAT YOU'RE TALKING ABOUT.
WHY DON'T YOU ASK KANAME?
GULP

9番目のムサシ

Mission 19: Omega - Part 2

......
WILL YOU PLEASE RETURN THAT PAGE?

I TOLD YOU BEFORE!
I DON'T KNOW WHAT YOU'RE TALKING ABOUT!

WHY WON'T YOU GIVE IT BACK?
YOU DON'T NEED IT.

YOU DON'T KNOW WHEN TO GIVE IT A REST.
HAVE YOU BOTHERED TO LOOK FOR IT ELSEWHERE? WHY DON'T YOU GET THAT U.B.--OR WHATEVER IT WAS CALLED--TO LOOK FOR IT?

I GOT YOU INTO THIS. SO, I HAVE A DUTY TO GET YOU OUT.
I WOULD LIKE TO KEEP THIS A PRIVATE AFFAIR.
......
OH YEAH? IT DOESN'T GET ANY MORE PRIVATE THAN THIS! IN FACT, IT'S A JOKE, IF YOU ASK ME!
......
PRIVATE?!
TAKE A LOOK AROUND YOU! LOOK WHERE WE ARE!
?
HE SAID THE SAME THING.
WHY DO YOU BOYS WORRY ABOUT WHERE YOU ARE?
PERSONALLY, I THINK IT'S A GOOD SPOT. IT'S PRIVATE.
JUST GET OUTTA HERE, OKAY?!
CREAK

TRUE.
IT'S A FREE PERIOD NEXT.
REAL-LY?
YEAH. SWEET.
HUH?!
WAIT A SEC...
SHINO'S A GIRL, RIGHT?
She's totally nuts.
And, what was all that about?
"He said the same thing?"
Who's "he?" And, what were they doing in the guy's bathroom?!
"You boys?!"
This is definitely *not* cool! In fact, it sucks!

"Admit it. You like Shino-hara."
I DO NOT!

"You're telling me Miss Special Weapons and Tactics made mincemeat out of seasoned mercenaries?"

"You like her, don't you?"

There's no way she's getting that page back! No way!

"You really do believe that fantasy of yours, don't you?"
"You also believe she's gonna split the second she gets that page back."

WHAT ARE YOU DOING, SCREAMING IN THE HERE?
What's your deal?
YOU FREAKED ME OUT. NOW IT'S ALL OVER MY PANTS.

YEAH... UM... RIGHT... YOUR PANTS?
COUGH
YEAH, ANYWAY, UM... WHERE'S KANAME?

NO. HE HA TO SPLIT EARLY.
HIS YOUNGER BRO' TOOK A TURN FOR THE WORSE.
His brother? Makoto?!
Kaname!
ICU
INTENSIVE CARE UNIT
HE HAD A VERY BAD ATTACK AFTER LUNCH.
THEY MANAGED TO STABILIZE HIM--ONLY BARELY. HE ISN'T OUT OF THE WOODS YET.
WHERE'S THE OLD MAN?
ON HIS WAY BACK FROM A BUSINESS TRIP.
OH.

THE DOCTOR SAYS WE HAVE TO DECIDE SOON.
I JUST WISH HE'D WAKE UP.
THEN...
THEN...
THEN...
THEN I'D LET HIM DO WHATEVER HE WANTS. TAKE HIM WHEREVER HE WANTS TO GO. (SOB)
MOM!
WE SHOULD'VE LOOKED FOR A BETTER HOSPITAL!
A HOSPITAL WHERE HIS ODDS OF SURVIVING COULD'VE BEEN 55 OR EVEN 60 PERCENT!
THAT'S IMPOSSIBLE.
BECAUSE WE'RE SO HELPLESS, MAKOTO IS GOING TO--
GET A GRIP ON 'OURSELF!
M!
THIS IS A GOOD HOSPITAL, AND THE DOC'S GOOD, TOO.
YOU DID WHAT YOU COULD.
MAKO-TO?
HUH?

Makoto.
"I can get your bro' transferred."
"If it's all the same, wouldn't a hospital with the latest and greatest be more reassuring?"
"Think about it. It's for family."
"You won't have to worry about the bills."
KANAME?

HUH? OH, WHAT?
I SHOULDN'T HAVE BECOME ALL UPSET.
MAKOTO LOOKS A LOT BETTER NOW.
And, Makoto...
YOU'D BETTER GO ON HOME. YOU HAVE SCHOOL TOMORROW.
BUT, MOM--
SHUSH. YOUR FATHER WILL BE HERE SOON.
IF THAT'S WHAT YOU WANT.
Mom, you're wasting away.

GREAT NEWS. ♪ ♪
YOU KNOW ASAMI'S BUD, NAKAMURA?
WELL, HIS LITTLE BRO'S IN REALLY BAD SHAPE.
OH YEAH?
STILL NOT GONNA GIVE UP?
OF COURSE NOT!
I WANT THAT LITTLE MOUTHPIECE WORKED GOOD.
NOTHING'S GONNA STOP ME FROM THAT. *NOTHING.*
YEAH, BUT NAKAMURA AIN'T PLAYING ALONG AT ALL.
MAYBE IT WASN'T SUCH A HOT IDEA USIN' HIS BRO' AS BAIT.
YOU'RE WRONG.
IT'S WORKING ALL RIGHT. OTHERWISE, WHY DIDN'T HE TELL ASAMI WHAT REALLY HAPPENED?
HE'S MULLING IT OVER.

HE'S SERIOUSLY CONSIDER-ING SELLING ASAMI OUT.
JUST SUPPOSE IT WORKS AND YOU ACTUALLY DRAW ASAMI OUT.
WHAT ABOUT BUTCH THAT'S ALWAYS HANGING AROUND HIM?
HAT'S THE ROB- EM.
WHAT DO WE DO WITH *HER*?
JUST WHO IS SHE? SHE'S GOT SEVERAL GOONS OF HER OWN.
THEY AREN'T FROM OUR SCHOOL. I'VE NEVER SEEN THEM AROUND.
SO, HERE'D Y COME ROM?

MAYBE THEY'RE PA OF A GANG
MAY-BE.
SO? THEY'RE STILL TEENS.
IT'S JUST A NUMBERS GAME. WITH ENOUGH PEOPLE, WE CAN DEAL WITH THEM.
SO, KAZ? I'M SURE YOU'RE GOOD FOR THAT.
WELL YEAH
COUPLE A GUYS I USED TO HANG WITH HEAD UP THEIR OWN OUTFITS.
MAKE A DEAL WITH THEM.
WITH THEM, BUTCH WILL BE EASY ENOUGH TO DEAL WITH.
FIGHT FIRE WITH FIRE, I SAY.
KANAME?!

SO HOW WAS MAKOTO?
SHOULD YOU EVEN BE HERE?
HE'S STABLE.
HE'S FINE.
PHEW
THAT'S A RE-LIEF.
YOU WERE QUIET ALL MORNING, SO I THOUGHT IT WAS PRETTY SERIOUS.
I'M GLAD TO HEAR IT, DUDE.
GACHA
HUH?
THEY'RE STILL NOT BACK?
LIKE ALWAYS.
THEY'RE FOOLIN' AROUND SOME-WHERE.

I KNOW YOU WON'T BELIEVE THIS.
BUT, SHINOHARA'S REALLY SPECIAL.
I KNOW I DIDN'T DREAM WHAT HAPPENED THIS SUMMER.
I AIN'T LYING OR DREAMING WHEN I SAY SHE'S WITH U.B., SOME INTERNATIONAL ORGANIZATION.
I'M SURE SHE IS SPECIAL-- EVEN IF SHE WASN'T IN THIS U.B.
REALLY? NOTHING LIKE, SHE LOOKS LIKE A GUY OR SHE'S TOTALLY OUT THERE?
YEAH.
YEAH. SURE, SURE.
I KNEW I COULD COUNT ON A FRIEND TO UNDERSTAND.
IT MEANS A LOT.
......

IT'S PRETTY OBVIOUS SHE ISN'T ORDINARY.
She's a chick, but she's bossing all these goons around.
Normal girls don't do that.
ONE MORE THING.
IT'S ABOUT *UCHIDA*.
WHAT ARE YOU TALKING ABOUT?
IT'S... UM...
"Call Asami out."
"Do that, and I'll get your little bro' into a good hospital."
WHAT ARE YOU HIDING FROM ME?
WHY DOES HE NEED TO TALK TO YOU THEN?

LUNCH BREAK'S OVER.
I HAVE TO GET GOING. THE PHYSICS TEACHER IS A REAL STICKLER FOR TIME.
STOP AVOIDING ME!
WHAT'S WRONG WITH YOU?! I'M NOT EVEN GETTING THROUGH TO YOU!
EVERY TIME I ASK, YOU WALK AWAY!
WHAT ARE YOU HIDING?!
SHUT UP! I SAID IT'S GOT NOTHING TO DO WITH YOU!
YOU WORRY ABOUT YOUR LITTLE SPY FRIEND! THAT'S WHAT YOU WANT, ISN'T IT?
MIND YOUR OWN BUSINESS!
SLAM!
KANAME?!
Kaname?

I MANAGED TO GET A HOLD OF THEM.
AND...?
THEY'RE GETTING THEIR GUYS TOGETHER.
RIGHT ON.
I ALSO ASKED THEM ABOUT THAT SHINOHARA. NO HARDCORE GANGSTERS CAME OUT OF THIS SCHOOL.
SO, THEY WERE CHOKED BIG TIME. SOME OUT-OF-TOWNERS WERE ON THEIR TURF.
WE GOT NOTHING TO WORRY ABOUT WITH BUTCH.
GOOD.
SO ALL WE HAVE TO DO IS GET ASAMI OUT IN THE OPEN.

ANYONE SEEN KANAME?
HE ALREADY SPLIT.
HE WHAT?
Without saying a word to me?!
What's that guy thinking?
He's been totally ignoring me!
I've been patient with him, and this is how he treats me?!
ASAMI.
GIVE IT A REST WILL YOU?
Can't you see I'm busy?
IT'S NOT THAT.
I THINK I SAW NAKAMURA BY THE LOCKERS.
OH.
WELL, THANKS.
YOU'RE WELCOME.

WHY'RE YOU FOLLOWING ME?
I'M NOT.
I'M GOING HOME, TOO.
SEE YOU.
BYE.
GRRRRR
?
WHY ARE YOU ANGRY?
WHAT'S THE POINT IN BEING DESIRED-- BY OTHER GIRLS?!
TRY CLUEING THEM IN YOU'RE A GIRL.
EVERYONE THINKS YOU'RE A GUY.
2-3
2-4
2-5
2-6

WHAT ARE THEY DOIN TO KANAME?
SH. WAIT.
THIS WAY.
SO? DID YOU THINK IT OVER?
I ALREADY TOLD YOU MY ANSWER.
THINK YOU SHOULD BE SAYING THAT?

I KNOW YOUR BRO'S NOT IN GOOD SHAPE.
THINK IT OVER.
I'M NOT ASKING YOU TO DO MUCH. CALL ASAMI OUT FOR US.
TELL HIM TO COME TO THAT CONSTRUCTION SITE NEAR YOUR PLACE AT EIGHT TOMORROW NIGHT.
DO THAT, AND EVERYTHING'S TAKEN CARE OF.
YOUR BRO' WILL HAVE A PRIVATE ROOM IN A GOOD HOSPITAL--*FREE*. HE CAN EVEN HAVE HIS OPERATION THERE.
IT'S A GOOD DEAL.
HOW...
YES?
HOW LOW ARE YOU WILLING TO STOOP?

SLAP
I DON'T SELL MY FRIENDS OUT!
I'M NOT LIKE YOU, YOU SCUMBAG!
LEAVE ME ALONE!
HEY, JERKWAD! HE'S SHOW-ING--
FOR-GET IT.
IT'S TEARING HIM UP.
I'VE SAID MORE THAN ENOUGH.
ALL WE HAVE TO DO IS WAIT THEN.
EITHER WAY, HE LOSES.
HA HA HA HA HA
......
WHAT WAS ALL THAT ABOUT?

WHAT'S GOING ON?
WHAT WERE THEY TALKING ABOUT?
THEY WERE STILL AT IT.
"STILL?"
WHAT DO YOU KNOW THAT I DON'T?!
I SAW THE SAME SCENE PLAYED OUT A FEW DAYS AGO.
WHY DIDN'T YOU TELL
IT'S A *PRIVATE* MATTER.
YOU COULD'VE DEALT WITH IT!
WHY DIDN'T YOU *DO* SOMETHING ABOUT IT?!
I DID, IN FACT. THAT WAS BECAUSE I GOT HIM INVOLVED.
BUT, I WON'T DO MORE.

I DON'T WANT TO BECOME INVOLVED ANYMORE THAN I HAVE TO.
WE TRY TO STAY CLEAR OF PROBLEMS AT THE CIVILIAN LEVEL.
I DON'T WANT TO DO SOMETHING UNNECESSARY AND ENDANGER THE ENTIRE MISSION.
......
You... you...
RUSTLE RUSTLE
NAKAMURA KANAME?
ABSENT?
Kaname!

HELLO? THIS IS THE DISTRICT GENERAL HOSPITAL.
NAKAMURA KANAME? YOU MEAN MAKOTO'S BROTHER?
NO. HE HASN'T BEEN BY TODAY.
RAAAH
HEY! NO SCREAM-ING IN THE HALLS.
CLICK
HUH
DUCK
SO? HOW'D IT COME TOGETHER?
EVERYTHING'S READY. WE GOT MORE THAN ENOUGH GUYS.
SUPPOSE ASAMI DON'T SHOW?
THEN WE UGLY UP NAKAMURA.
THE LOOK ON ASAMI'S FACE WILL BE PRICELESS.

OF CALLS: 1
ASAMI TAKERU

SQUEEZE
JUST WHERE ARE YOU GOING?
SHINO-HARA?

IT'S PRETTY OBVIOUS, ISN'T IT?! THE CON-STRUCTION SITE!
KANAME'S NOWHERE! SO, HE HAS TO BE THERE!
UCHIDA IS ALREADY THERE WITH A LOT OF "FRIENDS."
I WOULDN'T GO THERE.
WHAT'S YOUR PROB-LEM?!
DON'T YOU STICK UP FOR YOUR CLASS-MATES?!
DON'T YOU CARE IN THE LEAST?!
......
I WAS STUPID FOR EVEN ASKING!
WAIT.
WHAT?!

RETURN THE PAGE AND I WILL HELP.
THOSE ARE MY CONDITIONS.
DEAL?
You evil, conniving...
ALL RIGHT THEN! YOU'LL GET THAT STUPID PAGE BACK!
YOU'LL GET IT BACK, SO DO SOMETHING!
SIXTY-FOUR?
ROGER.

RIGHT HERE.
INITIATE THE OPERATION.
ROGER.
MOBILIZE AND DEPLOY THE TROOPS.
UH... HEY.
WHAT WAS ALL THAT?
WHAT ARE YOU PLAN-NING?
NOT TO WORRY. WE'RE JUST GOING TO SCARE THEM.
IT'S THE MOST EFFECTIVE WAY.
UM... SCARE THEM?
AN EYE FOR AN EYE.
A TOOTH FOR A TOOTH.

FIGHT FIRE WITH FIRE.
YO.
YOU ACTUALLY HAD THE GUTS TO COME HERE.

I DON'T SEE ANY SIGN OF ASAMI.
WHERE'S HE HIDIN'?
BUT, WHAT'S THIS?
HE AIN'T COMIN'.
I DIDN'T CALL HIM IN THE FIRST PLACE.
WHAT ARE YOU--DRUNK?!
OKAY.
I THINK YOU SHOULD CALL HIM, THOUGH.
OR ELSE, YOU'RE TAKING IT INSTEAD.

THEY'RE NOT TOO HAPPY THEY CAME ALL THE WAY FOR NOTHING.
I GUESS THEY'LL HAVE TO TAKE IT OUT ON YOU.
HOLD IT!
ASAMI?!
YOU IDIOT! WHAT ARE YOU DOING HERE?!
YOU'RE THE IDIOT!
WHO DO WE HAVE HERE?
FINALLY, ASAMI.
BEEN WAITIN' FOR YOU.

WISH
OH-HO. THEY SHOWED.
THESE THE PUNKS ON OUR TURF?!
SMIRK
SHALL WE BEGIN?
KA-SHIK
SHI! <YES!>
SHI! <YES!>
FLAP

GACHA
GACHA
SMIRK
GACHA

POW POW POW
WAUGH!
THEY'RE...
THEY'RE REAL!
THEY'RE NOT JUST ANY GANG!
IT'S...IT'S...
IT'S A CHINESE TRIAD!

WAUGH WAUGH WAUGH
WHAT DID YOU JUST DO?
DIDN'T I TELL YOU? SHE AIN'T NORMAL.
I didn't think she'd go this far, though.
So, it was true.
Everything Asami said was true.
NAKA-MURA?
THERE'S SOMETHING I'D LIKE TO SHOW YOU.
THERE'S A CAR WAITING OUT FRONT IF YOU'RE WILLING TO COME.

UNITED STATES AIR FORCE
Yokota Air Base
HEY...THIS IS AN AMERICAN AIR FORCE BASE.
WE'RE ACTUALLY GOING IN?
THERE IT IS.

KANA-
ME!
MOM?
DAD?
IT'S ONE OF OURS. IT'S FULLY EQUIPPED.
THINK OF IT AS A FLYING HOSPITAL.

YOUR BROTHER AND PARENTS ARE GETTING ON BOARD.
THEY'RE GOING TO GERMANY.
GER-MANY?
WE CAN FINALLY OPERATE!
A FAMOUS DOCTOR IN GERMANY IS GOING TO OPERATE!

THE DOCTOR AT THE HOSPITAL SUDDENLY RECOMMENDED IT! HE SAID HE WAS ABLE TO GET THROUGH TO HIM!
HE ARRANGED FOR THE AIRPLANE AND EVERYTHING! AND, WE DON'T HAVE TO WORRY ABOUT THE BILLS!
MAKOTO'S GOING TO BE FINE!
WE'RE READY.
WE'RE OFF, OKAY, DEAR?
MIND THE HOUSE AND DON'T FORGET TO STUDY.
VEEEEEEEEEEEEE

YOU...

YOU SET ALL THIS UP, DIDN'T YOU?

THE WORLD'S LEADING CARDIOLOGIST IS GOING TO SEE HIM.

HE GUARANTEED A 90 PERCENT CHANCE OF SUCCESS.

THINK OF IT AS A LITTLE PERK.

CERTAIN ADVANTAGES COME WITH THIS JOB.

YEAH. SEEMS IT.
SEE? I TOLD YOU!
SHE AIN'T NORMAL!

PRETTY SPECIAL I'D SAY.
GULP
NOW THEN.
WHERE IS THAT SHEET?
THAT SHEET... RIGHT... HEH.
ALL RIGHT, ALL RIGHT.
YOU WANT IT BACK?! WELL, HERE.
IT'S RIGHT...

HERE?
WELL?
I DON'T HAVE IT! IT'S GONE!
I'M SITIVE I IT IN THIS OCKET!
THAT SHEET?
YOU SAID YOU DIDN'T WANT TO LOSE IT, SO YOU LEFT IT ON THE DESK BACK AT THE CLUB.
...... RIGHT.
CHILLLLLLLLL
COOL.

WHAT IS IT?
I WENT BY THE OMEGA ROOM. THIS WAS SITTING ON ONE OF THE DESKS.
INTERESTING WOULD BE AN UNDER-STATEMENT.
IS IT WORTH ANYTHING?
A LOT, I'D SAY.
WHAT ARE WE WAITING FOR?
End of Mission 19: Omega - Part 2

End of Musashi #9, vol. 8

CHECK OUT THIS NEW TITLE!

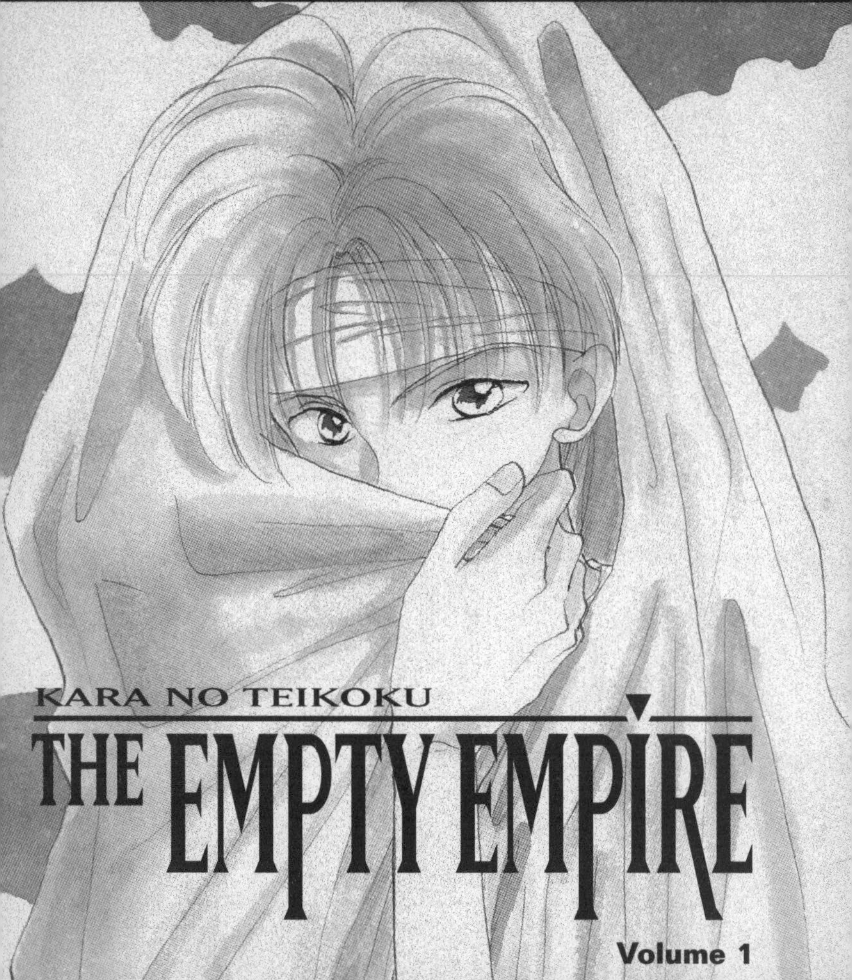

KARA NO TEIKOKU

THE EMPTY EMPIRE

Volume 1

By Naoe Kita. A boy with no memory finds himself on the run. Rescued by a girl who is a guardian of the imperial palace, he is named "Rose" due to the mysterious, flower-shaped scar on his forehead. Rose bears a striking resemblance to the recently departed, beloved emperor and may in fact be his clone! One faction wants the reluctant Rose to assume the mantle of leadership; another wants to put their own clone on the throne instead...and eliminate Rose in the process!

IF YOU LIKE MUSASHI #9, YOU'LL LOVE THESE SERIES, TOO!

By Keiko Yamada
2 Volumes Available

By Yasuko Aoike
6 Volumes Available

By Saki Hiwatari
3 Volumes Available

By You Higuri
5 Volumes Available

For more information and sneak previews, visit cmxmanga.com. Call 1-800-COMIC BOOK for the nearest comics shop or head to your local book store.

MUSASHI #9 Volume 8, published by WildStorm Productions, an imprint of DC Comics, 888 Prospect St. #240, La Jolla, CA 92037. English Translation © 2006. All Rights Reserved. English translation rights in U.S.A. arranged with Akita Publishing Co., Ltd., Tokyo, through Tuttle-Mori Agency, Inc., Tokyo. The stories, characters, and incidents mentioned in this magazine are entirely fictional. Printed on recyclable paper. WildStorm does not read or accept unsolicited submissions of ideas, stories or artwork. Printed in Canada.

DC Comics, A Warner Bros. Entertainment Company.

Tony Ogasawara – Translation and Adaptation
William F. Schuch – Lettering
Larry Berry – Design
Jim Chadwick – Editor

ISBN:1-4012-0859-2
ISBN-13: 978-1-4012-0859-2

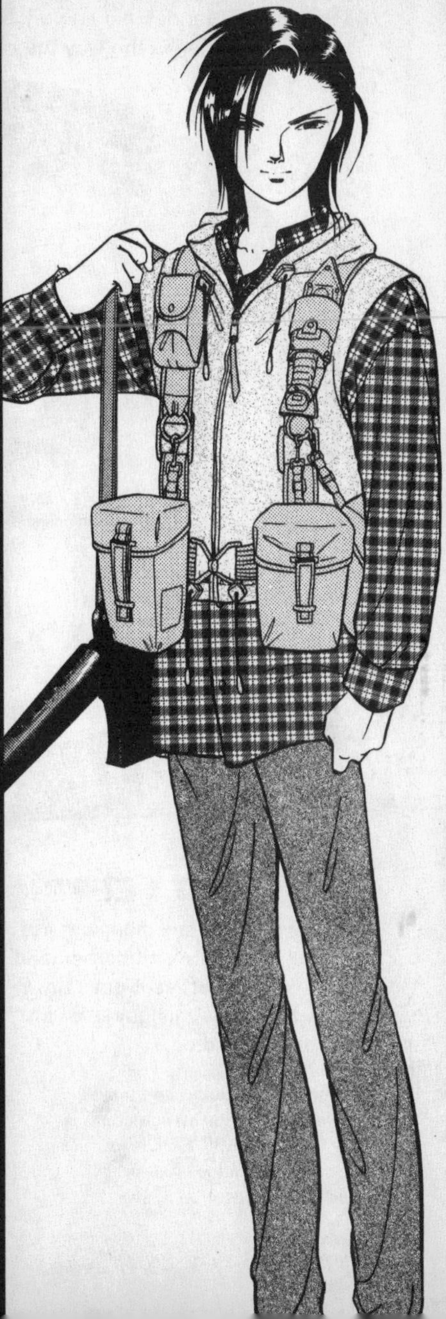

All the pages in this book were created—and are printed here—in Japanese RIGHT-to-LEFT format. No artwork has been reversed or altered, so you can read the stories the way the creators meant for them to be read.

FLIP IT!

RIGHT TO LEFT?!

Traditional Japanese manga starts at the upper right-hand corner, and moves right-to-left as it goes down the page. Follow this guide for an easy understanding.

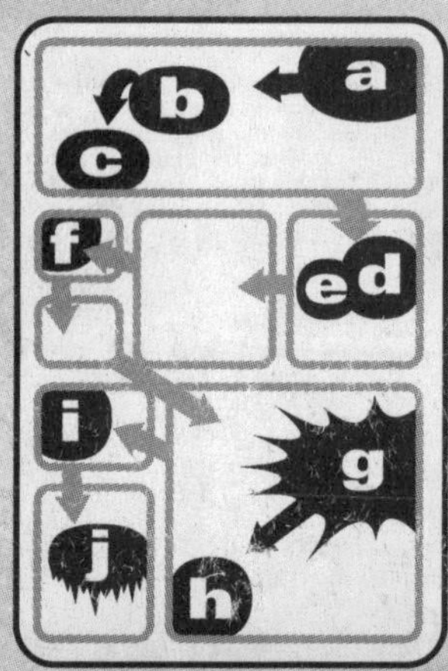

For more information and sneak previews, visit cmxmanga.com. Call 1-800-COMIC BOOK for the nearest comics shop or head to your local book store.